THE MUSEUM OF ANATOLIAN CIVILIZATIONS

EUROPEAN
MUSEUM OF THE YEAR
AWARD

The Museum of Anatolian Civilisations, Ankara, Turkey

The Committee would like to take this opportunity of expressing its
regard for the outstanding achievements and contribution to
museum progress of

Winner of the 1997 Award

and has great pleasure in making this Presentation as a
permanent record of its esteem.

Kenneth Hudson

KENNETH HUDSON
Director

THIS GUIDE BOOK HAS BEEN PREPARED BY MEMBERS OF STAFF AT
THE MUSEUM OF ANATOLIAN CIVILIZATIONS
AS A SERVICE TO THE MUSEUM.

DÖNMEZ OFFSET MÜZE ESERLERİ TURİSTİK YAYINLARI
G.M.K.Bul. 77/E Maltepe · 06570 ANKARA
Tel: 0.312 229 79 61 · Fax: 0.312 229 25 69

1. Oil painting of old Ankara by an unknown artist, 17th century, Rijks Museum Amsterdam. Dimensions 200 x 117 cm.

2. Aerial view of the historic area around the Museum of Anatolian Civilizations.

3. Views of the Museum buildings at the beginning of the 20th century and after its restoration.

THE HISTORY OF THE MUSEUM BUILDINGS

The Anatolian Civilizations Museum is located in the district called Atpazarı ("the horse market") to the south of Ankara Castle. The Museum occupies two Ottoman buildings which have been renovated and altered to suit their new role. One of them is the Mahmut Pasha Bedesten and the other is the Kurshunlu Han.

It is believed that the Bedesten (part of a bazaar where valuable goods were stored) was built between 1464 and 1471 by Mahmut Pasha, the grand vizier of Sultan Mehmet the Conqueror. There is no inscription on the building. Documentary sources, however, indicated that Ankara "sof" (cloth made from goat or camel hair) was distributed from here. The building has a plan of standard type. There is a covered rectangular area with 10 domes in the middle. There is a surrounding vaulted arcade, occupied by shops arranged so that those of the same trade face each other.

Recent research into the land registers and judicial records of the Ankara province show that Kurshunlu Han was built by Mehmet Pasha who succeeded Mahmut Pasha to the post of grand vizier in the reign of Sultan Mehmet. He held the post until 1470, and he founded the Han to provide revenue for his soup-kitchen or the poor and needy in the Usküdar, where finally he was buried. The building lacks an inscription, but during restoration work carried out in 1946 coins of Sultan Murat II were found, proving that the Han was in existence by the first half of the 15th century. The building has a typical plan for a Han of the Ottoman Period. In the middle there is a courtyard. It is surrounded by a series of rooms in two storeys. There are 28 rooms on the ground floor and 30 on the first. All of the rooms have fireplaces. In the basement of the west and south sides of the building there is a L-shaped stable. There are 11 shops on the north side, 9 on the east and 4 facing each other in the open - ended vaulted antechamber.

The two buildings, which are used as a Museum today, fell out of use after a fire in 1881.

4. Aerial view of Ankara Castle and environs.

5. View of Akkale, formerly used as a museum for many years.

THE HISTORY OF THE MUSEUM

The first Museum in Ankara was established in 1921 by Mübarek Galip Bey, Director of Cultural Affairs, in one of the towers of Ankara Castle called the "Akkale". In addition, objects were also collected together at the Temple of Augustus and at the Roman Baths. As a result of a suggestion by Atatürk that a Hittite Museum should be established, objects belonging to the Hittite period that were located in other museums began to be sent to Ankara. The need thus arose for a larger museum. Dr. Hamit Zübeyir Koşay, Director of Cultural Affairs, submitted a proposal to Saffet Arıkan, the Minister of Education, stating that the Mehmet Pasha Bedesteni and the Kurshunlu Han could be used after some essential alterations as a Museum. This proposal was accepted and work started in 1938. Restoration was only completed in 1968. However, after the work on the domed central room of the Bedesten had been partly finished in 1940, a start was made on the arrangement of display objects under the direction of Prof. H. G. Guterbock. This display was opened to the public in 1943 while other parts of the museum were still under construction. The restoration project of this part was drawn up by the architect, Macit Kural, and the restoration itself was carried of by the architect, Zühtü bey, after competitive bidding. In 1948 the museum moved into the four rooms at the Kurshunlu Han, the restoration of which was then finished, there by leaving the building at Akkale as a depot. The restoration and display projects of the shops around the domed area were drawn and carried out by İhsan Kıygı, an architect at the Monuments Department. Five of the shops were left in their original condition, but the walls between other shops were removed and a large surrounding corridor was created as an exhibition area. The Museum building took its present form in 1968. Today the Kurshunlu Han is used as the administration section. Located there are study rooms, the library, a conference hall, a laboratory and workshops. The Mahmut Pasha Bedesteni is used as the public display area.

The Anatolian Civilizations Museum is among the leading museums of the world on account of its unique collections of material. The archaeology of Anatolia from the Palaeolithic Age to the present day is displayed by periods in chronological order in the pleasant ambience of Ottoman surroundings.

6. View of the Museum entrance.

7. View of the Neolithic Age display.

8. General view of the Phrygian room.

9. Half-sized reconstruction of Midas' wooden burial chamber.

10. General view of the Phrygian room from the Urartian room.

11. View of the central gallery area, where stone orthostat blocks and statues are displayed in their original arrangement.

12. View of the Classical Period display.

13. General view of the gallery where exhibits from Ankara are displayed.

14. General view of the Karain Cave.

THE PALAEOLITHIC AGE

The Palaeolithic Age or Old Stone Age began nearly 2 million years ago and lasted until 10.000 years ago. This is a general time - scale, valid for the world as a whole, but the exact length of the Palaeolithic Age varies from region to region. During this long period of prehistory early man first appeared. By producing the first tools he took the first, all important step on the road of evolution.

Palaeolithic Man, whose existence was constantly threatened by natural and environmental pressures, lived in hunting and gathering groups. Mankind did not yet know how to grow crops but survived by gathering wild vegetables, fruits and roots and by eating the meat of the animals he hunted. As a result of climatic and environmental changes people migrated from one place to another, following the animals they hunted and searching for new supplies of food.

They used caves and rock shelters as dwellings whenever they could find such places. Elsewhere they made shelters for themselves as best they could out in the open.

The Palaeolithic Age is divided into three phases, Lower, Middle and Upper, each distinguished by a number of characteristic features.

Drawing on his limited intelligence, Lower Palaeolithic Man started to fashion stone into simple tools and weapons in order to protect himself from wild animals, to feed himself, to hunt and at times to fight his fellows. The stone tools were usually shaped by using other harder stones, or were stones which required very little reworking.

The temperate climate of the Lower Palaeolithic Age was replaced in the Middle Palaeolithic Age by drier, harsher weather with heavy snowfalls, which led to a glacial period. This brought about a change in man's life - style and technological abilities. The most striking change in technology is shown in the stone tools. The rough, double - sided stone tools of the Lower Palaeolithic Age were replaced by tools which were properly worked. There were also innovations in the shapes of the tools.

By means of retouching on the edges, Palaeolithic Man obtained end, cutting, and scraping tools. In the Middle Palaeolithic Age Neanderthal Man was able to hunt the larger animals such as mammoths, rhinoceroses and deer. Although he used only hand - held weapons, it does prove that he had the necessary skills and tools for hunting.

During the Middle Palaeolithic Age we also find evidence for ritual practices. For example, graves comprising one or two pits were found to have places next to them where food was deposited. These show us something of the burial - customs of Neanderthal Man.

In the Upper Palaeolithic Age, when the weather again turned cold and dry, Homo Sapiens, the ancestor of modern man, replaced Neanderthal Man. Homo Sapiens was more akin to modern, intelligent man.

Stone - cutting reached the peak of its technical skill in the Upper Palaeolithic Age. The classic double - sided tools (hand axes) which were used throughout the Lower Palaeolithic Age and for part of the Middle Palaeolithic Age were replaced by various types of tools made from flint, blades and flakes. Scrapers, stone drills, chisels, leaf - shaped arrowheads and weaving - shuttles are some examples of these tools. In the latter stages of the Upper Palaeolithic Age flakes with overlapping backs were found.

As well as stone tools, a great many tools were made from bone and horn. Also at this time a number of stone tools were made solely for use in shaping bone tools. This shows us that in the upper Palaeolithic Age the production of tools for making other tools had already started.

Another important development in the Upper Palaeolithic Age was the creation of artistic objects which relate to man's intellectual life. Multicolored paintings, sketches and scenes in low reliefs made on cave walls and on various objects, including statues, demonstrate the role of Palaeolithic Art in the history of art generally. In the Upper Palaeolithic Age the production of ornaments also started. We know that fish bones, shells and the bones and teeth of various animals were being used for ornaments by that time. The burial of the dead was arranged in an orderly fashion in this period.

Although the Palaeolithic Age in Anatolia is not fully understood from the results of excavation and survey work so far undertaken, it is clear from the finds of stone and bone tools, from the human, plant and animal remains, and from the artistic objects belonging to all the stages of the Palaeolithic Age that Anatolia was very densely populated throughout the Palaeolithic Age.

Karain is the only cave at present known in Anatolia where all the phases of the Palaeolithic Age are represented without interruption. This cave, which is 30 km northwest of Antalya, contains a number of "habitation levels" of the Lower Middle and Upper Palaeolithic Age. In addition to the stone and bone tools, the small portable artifacts, teeth and bone fragments of Neanderthal Man and Homo Sapiens have been unearthed together with a large quantity of burnt and unburnt bone.

Karain cave is an important site for the Palaeolithic Age is not just in Anatolia but in the whole of the Near East.

The reason for our ignorance about many aspects of the Palaeolithic Age in Anatolia is that accurate methods of dating have yet to be perfected. Research, however, continues on the material found at the excavations and surveys carried out along the Lower Euphrates in recent years and on the re - started excavations at Karain and Yarımburgaz They are producing important groups of evidence that will help to solve the remaining problems of stratigraphy and chronology in the Palaeolithic Age.

The finest exhibits of the Palaeolithic Age in the Museum come from Karain. They include a variety of stone tools - hand - axes, scrapers and arrowheads. The bone tools include awls, needles and ornaments. These objects were found in deposit layers measuring 10.5 meters deep which represent all the phases of the Palaeolithic Age.

15. Karain Cave, excavations in Locus E during 1986.

16. Karain Cave, Locus B.

17. View of the banks of the Euphrates river.

18. Two-sided flint tool from the Gaziantep area, Lower Palaeolithic Age.

19. Flint hand-axes of classic type from the Gaziantep area, Lower Palaeolithic Age.

20. Group of polished stone tools, flint, from the Üçağzlı Cave, Upper Palaeolithic Age.

21. A variety of flint tips from the Karain Cave, Middle Palaeolithic Age.

22. Aerial view of Çatalhöyük.

23. Reconstruction in the Museum of a Çatalhöyük house.

THE NEOLITHIC AGE

In man's prehistory the period in which the development of town - life started is known as the Neolithic Age. Neolithic Man knew how to produce food, but in the initial stages of this age the production of pottery was still unknown and so this period is called the "aceramic" period. At this time people used woven baskets, or wooden and stone containers. In Anatolia this phase has been identified at only a few sites. These first settled villages are represented by structures built in a fixed pattern, by stone or bone tools, and by weapons and certain ornaments.

The most highly developed Neolithic centre of the Near East and the Aegean World is Çatalhöyük, located 52 km southeast of Konya in the northern part of the Çumra Region. Excavations have revealed 10 different construction levels which, according to C14 dating, belonging to the period between 6800 and 5700 B.C. In these levels all the houses were built to a fixed pattern. This pattern was obtained by building rectangular houses next to each other around a courtyard. The houses were without stone foundations and had flat, mud - brick roofs. All of them were of the same plan: they had a large living - room, a storage room and a kitchen. The rooms were furnished with hearths, ovens and benches.

The main distinguishing features of the Çatalhöyük houses are the wall paintings and bulls head emblems on the walls. These decorations, most of which had cult associations, were not found in special buildings, but were located in a special area of the houses used for religious purposes. The bulls' heads were carved in high relief or made in the round, sometimes by covering an actual bull's head with clay. The wall paintings were on dull cream plaster and coloured in red, pink, brown, white and black. In addition to plain panels without any motifs, there were monochrome or polychrome geometric patterns, flowers, stars and solid circles. Scenes showing a number of different subjects were also produced. Among them were found representations of human hands, goddesses, human figures, hunting scenes and animal figures such as bulls, birds, vultures, leopards, deer, wild pigs, lions and bears. Other notable scenes include an erupting volcano behind a town, and a scene of human figures chasing away vultures that are pecking at headless skeletons.

These cult areas or shrines also depict a mother - goddess as a symbol of fertility. Figures of the mother - goddess were not only made of baked clay but also carved from stone. She is represented in various guises: as a young girl, an old woman or a woman giving birth to a child. Of these the figure of the mother - goddess giving birth to a child, supported on either side by two leopards, had a special significance. In addition to representations of the mother - goddess in figurines or in high reliefs, small terracotta models of animals were made as votive objects.

The hand - made Neolithic pottery at Çatalhöyük was usually brown, black and red in colour. The pottery shapes are mostly oval and, in the late phase of the Neolithic Age, decorated with simple geometric motifs.

Necklaces made of various stones and sea shells, obsidian mirrors and cosmetic articles show us how people adorned themselves at Çatalhöyük in the Neolithic Age. The earliest know surviving textile was found at Çatalhöyük. It can be seen from the wall - paintings that people used animal skins for clothing as well as textiles made of wool, animal hair or plant fibres. Stamp - seals, made of baked - clay or stone and decorated with geometric figures, provide the earliest envidence for claims of ownership in the Neolithic Age. Flint and obsidian were used to make various tools and weapons, while bone was used to make awls, needles and handles. Among the finds a flint dagger with a bone handle is particularly interesting. It was a grave gift. Although it was still not very common in this period, the working of copper and lead into artifacts was known. Trade also existed between settlements in Anatolia and the neighbouring regions.

The people of Çatalhöyük buried their dead under the floors of their houses. Children were buried under the floor of the room itself, while adults were buried, either individually or in groups, under the benches in the rooms. Grave gifts were placed beside the corpse.

Hacılar, which lies 25 km southeast of Burdur, is the second most important Neolithic site from which finds are displayed in the Museum. Only the four levels, IV to VI, belong to the Late Neolithic settlement (5700 - 5600 B.C.) out of the total of 9 levels that have been excavated. The houses at Hacılar, built on stone foundations with mud - brick walls, were like the Çatalhöyük houses but larger. They had red - painted plaster floors and walls. They had wooden posts supporting flat roofs and also stairs, showing that some of the structures were two - storied. In contrast to Çatalhöyük, the burials at Hacılar are extra - mural. Figurines of a seated or standing mother - goddess were found in nearly all of the houses.

The well - fired and glazed pottery of Hacılar is in red, brown and reddish yellow colours. The most interesting of the pottery exhibits are a red - coated glazed cup in the form of a female head and the rhytons in various animal shapes (deer, pigs, birds). Plant remains and sickles made of horn with flints embedded in one side reveal that the people of Hacılar knew about agriculture. Clay spindle whorls were also found, proving that textiles were being produced there.

24. Statuette of the Mother Goddess, terracotta, from Çatalhöyük, c.5,750 BC. Height 20 cm. The Goddess is seated on a throne, flanked by two sacred animals. She is represented as a woman in child-birth.

25. Relief of the Mother Goddess in lime plaster from Çatalhöyük, first half of the 6th millennium BC. Height 112 cm.

26. Four figures in high relief, stone, from Çatalhöyük, first half of the 6th millennium BC.
Height 11.6 cm.

27. Statuette of a goddess, black stone, from Çatalhöyük, first half of the 6th millennium BC. Height 15.5 cm.

28. Statuette of twin goddesses, marble, from Çatalhöyük, first half of the 6th millennium BC. Height 17.2 cm.

29. Statuette of the Leopard Goddess, limestone, from Çatalhöyük, first half of the 6th millennium BC. Height 11.8 cm.

30. Fragment of a statuette of a goddess, terracotta, from Hacılar, mid-6th millennium BC.
Height 5.3 cm.

31. Statuette of the Mother Goddess with child, terracotta, from Hacılar, mid-6th millennium BC.
Height 8.3 cm.

32. Statuette of a goddess, terracotta, from Hacılar, mid-6th millennium BC. Height 24 cm.

33. Small cooking pot and oven-stand, terracotta, from Çatalhöyük, 6th millennium BC.
Height 8.5 and 7.9 cm.

34. Vessel with four feet, terracotta, from Çatalhöyük, first half of the 6th millennium BC. Height 21.7 cm.

35. Vessel in the shape of a woman's head, terracotta, from Hacılar, mid-6th millennium BC. Height 11.1 cm.

36. Vessel in the shape of a deer, terracotta, from Hacılar, mid-6th millennium BC. Height 13.6 cm.

37. Vessel in the shape of a pig, terracotta, from Hacılar, mid-6th millennium BC.
Height 26 cm.

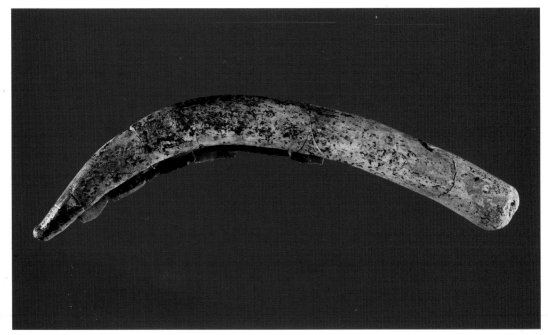

38. Horn sickle, from Hacılar, mid-6th millennium BC. Length 27.8 cm.

39. Wooden box containing stone and bone jewellery, from Çatalhöyük, first half of the 6th millennium BC.

42. Items of personal adornment made up of stone and bone beads, from Çatalhöyük, first half of the 6th millennium BC.

40. Obsidian mirror, from Çatalhöyük, first half of the 6th millennium BC. Diameter 6.6 cm.

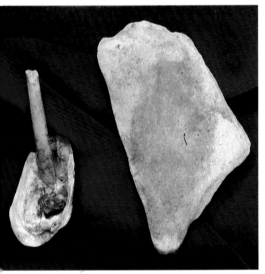

41. Cosmetic utensils, from Çatalhöyük, first half of the 6th millennium BC.

43. Artist's impression of a funerary rite conducted by priestesses dressed up in vulture costumes (based on finds from the excavations at Çatalhöyük).

44. Fresco of an ox hunt, painted plaster, from Çatalhöyük, 6th millennium BC.

45. Detail from the fresco of the deer hunt, depicting a hunter wearing a leopard skin, painted plaster, from Çatalhöyük, 6th millennium BC.

46. Artist's impres

47. The vulture fresco, painted plaster, from Çatalhöyük,
6th millennium BC.

48. Fresco depicting a plan of the city, painte

Çatalhöyük.   (Urs Landis)

49. The volcanic cone of Hasan Dağı, shown in the background of the City Plan Fresco. The mountain was an important source of obsidian for the inhabitants of Çatalhöyük.

from Çatalhöyük, 6th millennium BC.

50. Remains of shrines at Çatalhöyük, one of the oldest settlements in Anatolia,
now located 52 km east of Konya.

51. View of a Çatalhöyük shrine building.

52. View of a Çatalhöyük shrine building.

53. Fresco of a deer hunt, painted plaster, from Çatalhöyük, 6th millennium BC. Height 86 cm.

54. Relief depicting of a pair of leopards, painted plaster, from Çatalhöyük, 6th millennium BC.

55. Fresco of a wild donkey and birds, painted plaster, from Çatalhöyük, 6th millennium BC.

44

56. Stamp seal, terracotta, from Çatalhöyük, first half of the 6th millennium BC. Height 3.3 cm.

57. Bone belt clasp, from Çatalhöyük, 6th millennium BC. Height 5.2 cm.

58. Spear and arrow heads, obsidian, from Çatalhöyük, 6th millennium BC.

59. Mace heads, stone, from Çatalhöyük, 6th millennium BC.

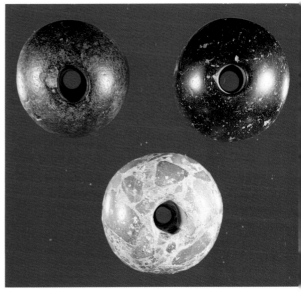

60. Spear and arrow heads, obsidian, from Çatalhöyük, 6th millennium BC.

61. Flint dagger with bone handle, from Çatalhöyük, 6th millennium BC. Length 19.5
and 10.3 (blade only) cm.

62. View of the excavations at Canhasan, an important Chalcolithic site, now situated 13 km south-east of Karaman on the
fringes of the Taurus Mountains. Excavations were carried out at Canhasan between 1962 and 1970.

THE CHALCOLITHIC AGE

This period is called the Chalcolithic Age because copper started to be used as well as stone. It is clear from sites such as Hacılar, Canhasan and Kuruçay that there is direct continuity from the Late Neolithic Age. In this period, as in the Neolithic Period, distinct regional characteristics were still dominant. It can be divided into three sub - periods: the Early, Middle and Late Chalcolithic Age.

The most advanced example of Early Chalcolithic Age culture in Anatolia is seen at Hacılar. The houses, which were square or rectangular, had stone foundations and flat roofs. Hacılar had the appearance of a town, with narrow streets running between the buildings and with a circuit of mud - brick fortifications. The entrances to the buildings, placed next to each other in a row, led from spacious courtyards. These large houses contained a small cult room, a work area, a well and a pottery workshop.

The most distinguishing feature of Hacılar is its handmade painted pottery. In the Early Chalcolithic Age, levels V to I at Hacılar (5400 - 4750 B.C.), bright, glazed monochrome pottery was produced in advanced forms and with advanced techniques. There is also a great increase in the quantity of polychrome decorated wares that were being produced. The painted pottery is decorated with geo- metric motifs in reddish brown on a pinkish yellow ground. Oval cups, globular jars, large vases, rectangular bowls, jars and jugs are among the different forms that are known. The majority of the terracotta figurines of the mother - goddess, which are a continuation from the Neolithic Age, represent the goddess seated in a more stylized fashion. The stone and bone artifacts, together with a small number of copper objects, show the same continuity of traditions.

Canhasan, which is located 13 km to the northeast of Karaman in the province of Konya, is another site where the three phases of the Chalcolithic Age have been found (levels III - I). Canhasan lies on the natural route between the Konya plain and the Çukurova. The settlement acted as a commercial and cultural exchange centre between these two areas. The houses at Canhasan were rectangular, like the ones at Hacılar, and had walls decorated with geometric motifs. The cream or buff - coloured hand - made pottery was thin - walled. In addition to the monochrome wares, there are types painted in red or black and others decorated with lines filled with a white substance. Among the most important metal objects found at Canhasan are a copper bracelet, a copper sceptre - or mace - head and some copper fragments.

Another major Late Chalcolithic centre is Beycesultan in western Anatolia, 5 km southeast of Çivril in the province of Denizli. Of the forty construction levels excavated those between level XL and XX (4000 - 3000 BC) have been recognized as belonging to the Late Chalcolithic Age. Some of the rectangular, mud - brick buildings resemble houses of the "megaron" type. These contain pillars that supported the walls, fireplaces, bench - seats adjoining the walls and plastered storage rooms. One important group of objects found inside a clay vessel at Beycesultan comprises a silver ring, copper implements, a dagger fragment and three metal needles. Most of the Late Chalcolithic pottery is plain ware in grey, black or brown coloured clay, but some vessels are decorated with white geometric motifs or linear patterns.

The earliest sites in north central Anatolia belong to the Late Chalcolithic Age. Finds from the Chalcolithic settlements at Alishar and Alacahöyük are on display in the Museum. Excavations at Alishar, which lies 67 km southeast of Yozgat, have revealed levels XIX - XII as belonging to the end of the Late Chalcolithic Age. At Alacahöyük in the province of Çorum the corresponding levels are numbered XV - IV. At both sites the remains of rectangular mud - brick buildings and examples of brown, black and dark grey pottery were found. Some of the monochrome wares are decorated with grooved or incised designs. These wares are usually found in the shape of fruit bowls, jugs and jars.

The Middle Chalcolithic Age of eastern Anatolia is represented at the Museum by finds from Tilkitepe to the southeast of Lake Van. In addition to obsidian tools and supplies of the raw material, painted pottery called "Halaf" ware was found at this site.

During the Chalcolithic Age burial customs differed from region to region in Anatolia. Both the intra - mural and the extra - mural traditions are seen, but in both cases the bodies are buried in jars or in stone sarcophagi. The burials included pottery, ornaments and weapons as gifts to the dead.

Although Anatolia was densely populated during the Chalcolithic Age, a uniform culture had not been imposed over the whole area. Because of its geographical location, Anatolia felt certain external influences at this time. In northwest Anatolia the cultures of the Balkans and the Aegean islands made their presence felt, while that of northern Mesopotamia influenced eastern and south - eastern Anatolia and that of north Syria spread into the Çukurova.

63. Painted statuette of the Mother Goddess, terracotta, from Hacılar,
second half of the 6th millennium BC. Height 8.8 cm.
(Stolen from the Anatolian Civilizations Exhibition held in Vienna, Austria, in 1990).

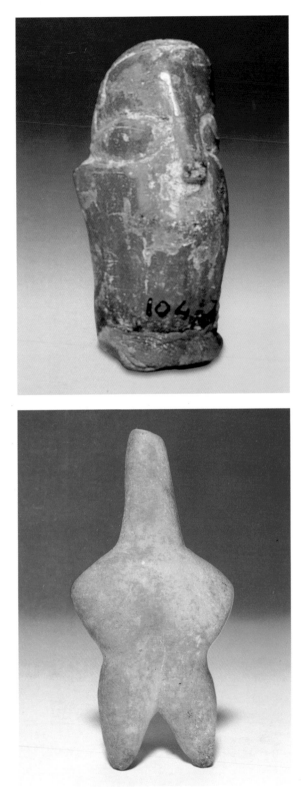

64. Head, terracotta, from Hacılar, second half of the 6th millennium BC. Height 4.4 cm.

65. Male figurine, marble, Canhasan, second half of the 5th millennium BC. Height 6.4 cm.

66. Female figurine, marble, Canhasan, second half of the 5th millennium BC. Height 10 cm.

67. Seated Mother Goddess, terracotta, Canhasan, first half of the 5th millennium BC. Height 32.5 cm.

68. Head, terracotta, Canhasan, second half of the 5th millennium BC. Height 8.7 cm.

69. Mace head, copper, Canhasan, first half of the 5th millennium BC. Diameter 5

70. Handled vessel with painted decoration, terracotta, Hacılar, second half of the 6th millennium BC. Height 11.8 cm.

71. Painted bowl, terracotta, Hacılar, second half of the 6th millennium BC. Height 8.8 cm.

72. Painted vessel, terracotta, Hacılar, second half of the 6th millennium BC. Height 11.2 cm.

73. Painted vase, terra-
cotta, Hacılar, sec-
ond half of the 6th
millennium BC.
Height 17 cm.

74. Painted vessel, ter-
racotta, Hacılar, sec-
ond half of the 6th
millennium BC.
Height 15.7 cm.

75. Large painted jar, terracotta, Canhasan, first half of the 5th millennium BC. Height 51 cm.

76. Painted vessel, terracotta, Canhasan, first half of the 5th millennium BC. Height 26.5 cm.

77. Aerial view of Alacahöyük.

THE EARLY BRONZE AGE

The Early Bronze Age started in Anatolia in the late 4th millennium or early 3rd millenium B.C. At that time the people of Anatolia knew how to make bronze by mixing copper and tin. From this alloy they made all of their weapons, ornaments and utensils. In addition to bronze, they also used copper, gold, silver and electrom (which is an alloy of gold and silver) to produce all the other objects they needed.

Many of the excavated sites, both large and small, show that people in the Bronze Age lived in settlements surrounded by defensive walls. These fortified cities appear to have contained buildings placed very close together. The houses, which reflect traditional Anatolian architecture, have stone foundations and mud - brick walls. They have square or irregular rooms furnished with hearths, furnaces and bench - seating.

Houses of the "megaron" type (long, one - roomed houses) can be seen at Beycesultan in the upper Meander valley. This type of building was in use for a long time in Anatolia.

The transition from the Late Chalcolithic to the Early Bronze Age was gradual and uninterrupted. The architecture of both town and village alike, the stampseals I and the idols continued to develop according to the local traditions. As in the Chalcolithic Age, the people engaged in crop cultivation and animal - husbandry made advances in the way they carried out these two all - important occupations. In addition, trade and metal - working also improved. Evidence for the growth in trade is seen in the distribution of goods over a large area. The working of different kinds of metal (gold, silver, copper, bronze, electron and even iron) was well known, and casting and hammering techniques had been developed. This is clear from the rich finds of metal, especially from graves, belonging to this period. Moulds used for casting have been found at sites, showing the advanced stage that had been reached in the technology of metal - working. The quantity and quality of the artifacts demonstrate that agriculture was not the only occupation at the time but that art and metallurgy were also important. The finds from Alacahöyük, Horoztepe, Eskiyapar, Kültepe, Mahmatlar, Kayapınar and even from Polatlı show very well that in this period metallurgy had gained as prominant a place as agriculture in man's activities. The manufacture and trade of metals had thus gained importance in this period. The largest centres of production were established in east and north - east Anatolia. If it had not been for this development in metalworking in Anatolia, it would have been very difficult to define the nature of trade in the Assyrian Colonies Period. The style of the metal statuettes, as well as reflecting man's beliefs and abstract concepts, is important since it demonstrates the development in metal - working and the artistic ability of the people of Anatolia. So, one can postulate the existence of a class of metal - working craftsmen in the Early Bronze Age.

An important centre that bears witness to the high level of civilization that was reached during the Early Bronze Age in Anatolia is Alacahöyük. The rich tombs discovered there are rectangular in shape, surrounded by stone walls and roofed with wooden beams. The skeletons are usually in the "hocker" position, with the knees drawn up to the stomach, and lie in the middle of the room together with the grave goods. Soil was placed on top of these wooden beams and plastered to make a flat roof, forming a house for the dead. The heads and legs of the oxen sacrificed during the funeral ceremony were left on the roof. Sheep and goats were also among the animals that were sacrificed. The sacrificial animals appear to have been associated with a feast for the dead. A dog was also left outside the tomb apparently as a guardian for the occupier. It is understood that the tombs, which continued in use for a long time, were intended for the royal princes who ruled the surrounding areas for several generations. The tombs belong to different occupation levels. Most of the grave goods are made from gold, silver, electron and bronze. There are also some objects made from amber, agate, rock crystal, iron and terracotta. The gifts found in the tombs include ornaments such as diadems, necklaces, needles, bracelets, buckles and earrings. Ceramic vessels were also found in the tombs. In addition, there are weapons made of bronze and gold, ritual solar discs, figurines of deer and bulls, goddess statuettes and sistra. The finds from Horoztepe, near Tokat, like the ones from Alacahöyük, demonstrate the wealth of the local rulers and the high level of metal - working that was reached in the northern regions. The finds from Eskiyapar, Kayapınar and Mahmatlar prove this from the point of view of the material, forms and symbolism of their artifacts. Parallels for some of the precious metal objects, idols and weapons are to be found made of fired clay, stone and base metal at almost every settlement.

From the excavations at Eskiyapar we can see that in central Anatolia precious objects were not only put in tombs as gifts for the dead but were also buried in the houses as treasure.

Bronze spear heads appear for the first time in Anatolia during the Early Bronze Age. Together with some types of axes, these spear heads and some of the other weapons have similarities to those in Mesopotamia and Syria. This can be seen from finds at Alacahöyük, Alişar Mahmatlar, Horoztepe and Dündartepe. The weapons excavated at İkiztepe, near Samsun, provide a good example of the art of metal - working at this period.

The Alacahöyük and Horoztepe tombs belong to Kings of Hatti, the people who lived there at that time. The civilization and art are, therefore, known by that name. Finds from these sites include bronze figurines of bulls and deer; similar figurines decorated with a coating of electron; solar - discs on which the sun and rays are worked together; statuettes of bulls and deer surrounded by a solar disc; and other discs decorated with bulls' horns. There ale also small female statues symbolizing fertility and motherhood, such as the statuettes from Horoztepe of a woman nursing her child, a small statuette from Hasanoğlan made of bronze, the head of which is gold and is plated with electron. All of these objects, like the sistra, are clearly associated with religious practices. Certain deities and divine symbols are first seen in the Early Bronze Age. For example, the motif of an eagle perched on a sistrum became very popular in the latter part of the period. These are the precursors of the solar discs, deer and bull cults and mother goddess statuettes found in the Assyrian Trade Colonies and Hittite Periods.

The handmade pottery of the Early Bronze Age is usually monochrome and only a very few examples have painted decoration. The decoration is usually in deep colours on a red or pale ground. The painted or incised decoration on the pottery always consists of geometric patterns. The principal types of pottery are beaked jugs, spouted teapots, large, black - glazed vessels decorated with grooves and geometric motifs in relief, one - handled bowls and cups, two - handled vases and jugs decorated with human faces. In the Late Bronze Age the forms of the fired - clay cups were very simple since they mostly take their shape from metal prototypes. At the end of the period there was a great increase in the number of the beaked pitchers, spouted and basket - handled teapots and angular cups and vases which imitated metal examples in clay. Most of these cup shapes are the first examples of the Hittite cup shapes seen in the later period.

In the Early Bronze Age the civilizations of western Anatolia, as in the other parts of Anatolia, had distinct cultural divisions and local characteristics. The topography of the region was one of the factors that gave rise to these differences. In the Museum the culture of west central Anatolia is represented by objects from Beycesultan and Yortan.

In the last phase of the Early Bronze Age trade links were established between central and western Anatolia. At this time the region of Troy was producing pottery in certain distinctive shapes, as well as ornaments made from precious metal. These items are to be found at important centres such as Beycesultan, Polatlı, Karaoğlan, Bozhöyük, Alişar, Kültepe, Gözlükule, Gedikli throughout central and south - east Anatolia. They are interesting because they indicate the area that was influenced by the culture of Troy II. Together with vessels decorated with stylised human faces, the hand-made, black cups of the Yortan type show that the common pottery forms of Western Anatolia had also reached the Ankara region. In addition to hand - made, monochrome vessels, wheel - made pottery also appeared in Central Anatolia in the last phase of the Early Bronze Age. There is also a new type of pottery which is known in archeological circles "intermediate" or Alişar III" ware. This new type of pottery is hand - made and painted. Examples of this culture are most often seen in the southern parts of Central Anatolia.

Fiddle - shaped statuettes, made of terracotta, bronze, silver or stone represent a new type of the mother goddess figures produced in the Neolithic and Chalcolithic Ages. Another new group of objects which are seen in the southern parts of Central Anatolia in the last phase of the Early Bronze Age, are the alabaster figurines with round bodies, and 1 to 4 heads. They are usually associated with the painted pottery in sacred deposits or in graves and, up to now, they have only been found at Kültepe. These figurines are usually naked and are decorated with concentric circles and geometric motifs on their middles. Others are decorated with small - scale reliefs, most particularly lion and human motifs. These figurines, whose sizes range between 5 and 30 cms in diameter, represent the fertility goddess. There are also flat - bodied idols and figurines of naked women that are usually shown sitting on thrones with their hands on their breasts. They are always made alabaster. They include examples that are worked out very naturally and show a stylistic development within a very short period of time. These finds from Kültepe have an important place in the evolution of the Anatolian style and shed light on a certain period in the history of local religions. They were produced in the last two centuries of the 3rd millennium B.C., together with the painted pottery of the Early Bronze Age.

The traditional Anatolian style stamp - seals that were used in the Neolithic Age continued through into the Early Bronze Age. They are made either of baked clay or of stone, but there are also a few made of metal. In this age the sizes of the stamp seals and of the motifs on them became smaller. The faces of the seals are convex and incised with geometric motifs. Loop - handles, with a vertical hole for a cord, continued in use. They also started to be put into graves as gifts in the Early Bronze Age.

The seals from Ahlatlıbel, Karaoğlan, Karayavşan are all very similar and a Mesopotamian influence can be seen on the seals found in southern Anatolia.

Among the Early Bronze Age finds there is a large quantity of spindle whorls, usually with some decoration, loom weights and wood spindles. They demonstrate that spinning and weaving were very much practiced in this period.

The cultures of eastern, central and western Anatolia had reached an advanced level of Civilization, each with its own local characteristics. External influences, internal relations between them and migrations did not effect these local characteristics. The most important feature of Anatolian civilization is that it preserved local characteristics throughout its history. In this period there were settlements throughout Anatolia, and the Anatolia peninsula was the culture and art centre of the ancient Near East. This period is represented by the rich finds in our Museum.

78. View of the excavations at Alacahöyük with the royal tombs.

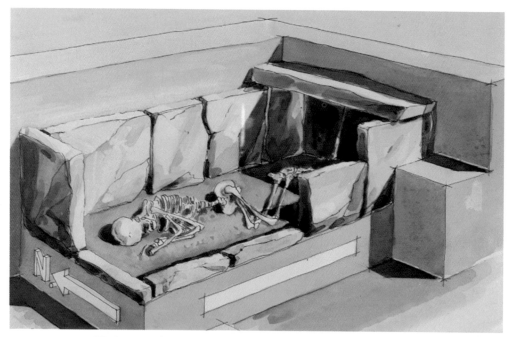

79. Drawing of a chest-like tomb, Alacahöyük excavations (by M. Akok).

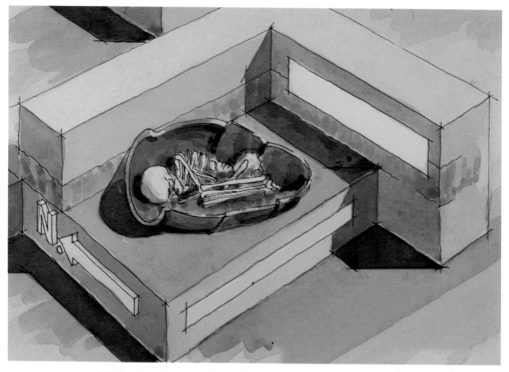

80. Drawing of a pithos burial, Alacahöyük excavations (by M. Akok).

81. Stag statuette, bronze, Alacahöyük, second half of the 3rd millennium BC. Height 52.5 cm.

82. Bull statuette, bronze, Alacahöyük, second half of the 3rd millennium BC. Height 37 cm. There is evidence from other finds that statuettes of bulls and stags were cult objects representing deities. It is thought that the cults associated with these animals that formed an important part of later religious beliefs started in the Early Bronze Age. This statuette must have been carried as a standard in religious processions.

83. Representation of an Early Bronze Age burial ceremony at Alacahöyük. The king lies on a bier awaiting burial in a tomb in which the queen has already been buried with her jewellery and other possessions.

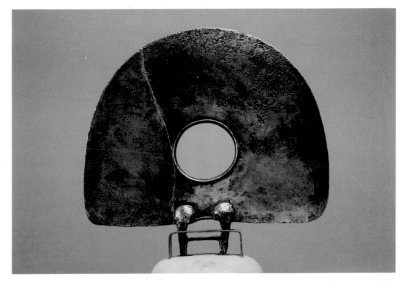

84. Ceremonial standard, silver, Alacahöyük, second half of the 3rd millennium BC.
Height 23.4 cm.

85. Sistrum, bronze, Horoztepe, end of the 3rd millennium BC. Height 25.5 cm.

86. Ceremonial standard, bronze, Alacahöyük, second half of the 3rd millennium BC. Height 24 cm. Such ritual objects frequently depict a sun disk flanked by bull's horns, although they come in many different designs. They are often found as grave gifts in the tombs of important people who were clearly buried with much pomp and ceremony. This standard was made by casting and beating.

87. Ceremonial standard, bronze, Alacahöyük, second half of the 3rd millennium BC. Height 18 cm.

88. Ceremonial standard, bronze, Alacahöyük, second half of the 3rd millennium BC. Height 34 cm.

89. Ceremonial standard, bronze, Alacahöyük, second half of the 3rd millennium BC. Height 23 cm.

90. Ceremonial standard, bronze, Alacahöyük, second half of the 3rd millennium BC. Height 34 cm.

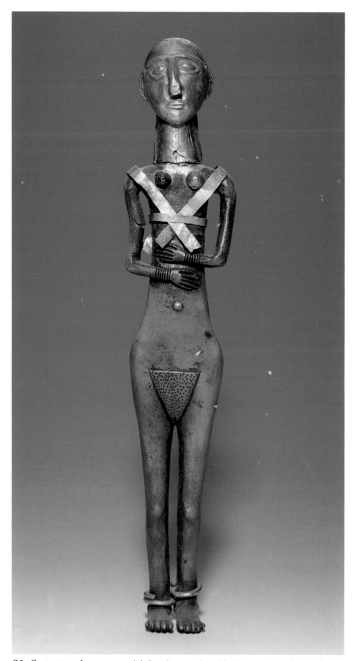

91. Statuette of a woman (idol), silver and gold, Hasanoğlan (stray find),
end of the 3rd millennium BC. Height 25 cm. Stylised female figurines
representing the Mother Goddess were made of precious metal, stone
and clay in the Early Bronze Age. Similar diagonal straps are found on
statuettes of the Anatolian Mother Goddess and so must be regarded
as significant part of her attire.

92. Statuette of a woman nursing a child, bronze, Horoztepe, end of the
3rd millennium BC. Height 21.5 cm.

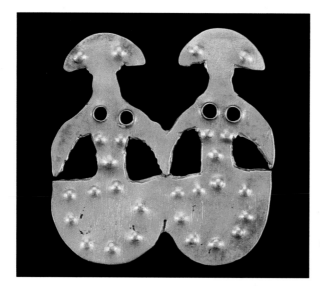

93. Twin idols, gold, Alacahöyük,
second half of the 3rd millennium BC. Height 4 cm.

94. Stylised female figurine (idol), silver,
Alacahöyük, second half of the 3rd
millennium BC. Height 10.6 cm.

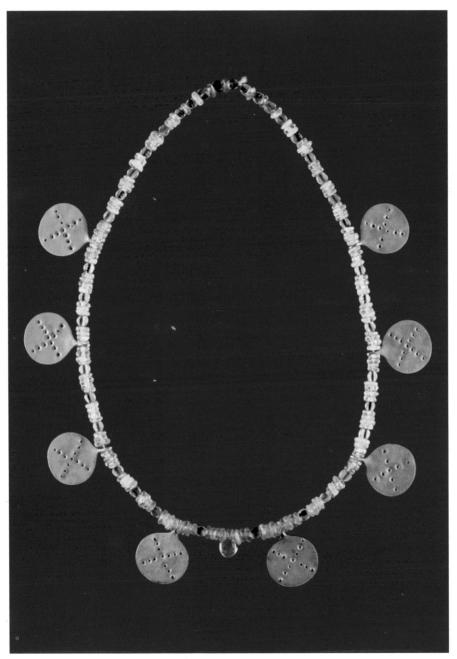

95. Necklace (modern arrangement), gold and crystal, Alacahöyük, second half of the 3rd millennium BC. Diameter (of disk-shaped ornaments) 3 cm.

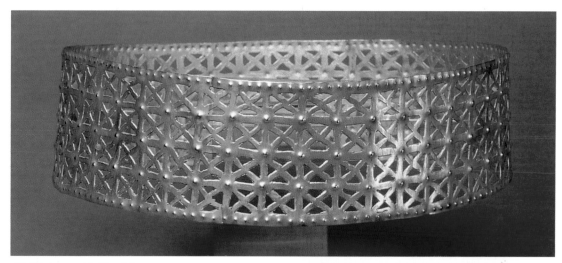

96. Diadem, gold, Alacahöyük, second half of the
3rd millennium BC.
Diameter 19.2 cm.

97. Hair ornament, gold,
Alacahöyük, second
half of the 3rd millenni-
um BC.
Diameter 3.5 cm.

98. Dress fastener and pin,
gold, Alacahöyük, sec-
ond half of the 3rd mil-
lennium BC.
Length 15.2 cm.

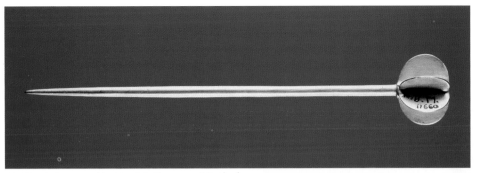

99. Headed pin, gold, Alacahöyük, second half of
the 3rd millennium BC. Length 18.5 cm.

100. Bracelet, gold, Alacahöyük, second half of the 3rd millennium BC. Diameter 6.5 cm.

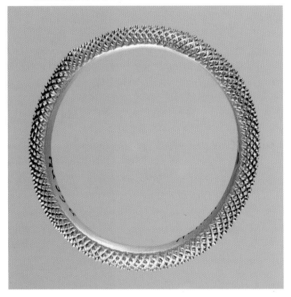

101. Diadem, gold,
Alacahöyük,
second half
of the 3rd
millennium BC.
Length 53 cm.

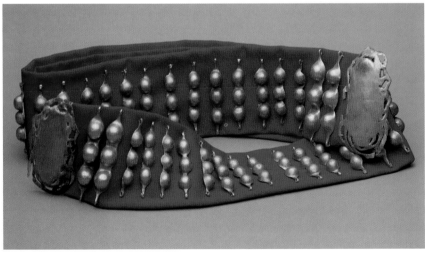

102. Belt ornaments,
gold, Alacahöyük,
second half
of the 3rd millen-
nium BC.
Width 4.4-5.6 cm.

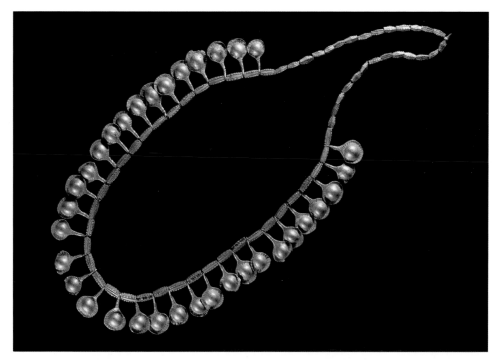

103. Necklace (modern arrangement), gold, Eskiyapar, second half of the 3rd millennium BC. Length 34 cm.

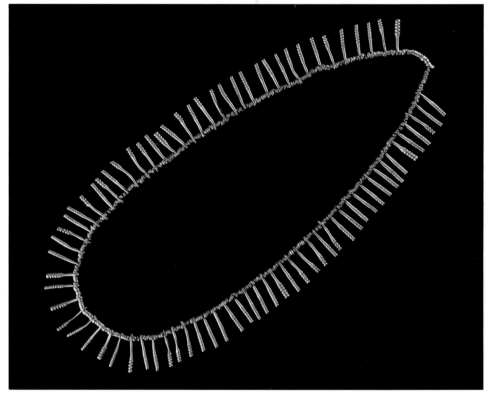

104. Necklace (modern arrangement), gold, Eskiyapar, second half of the 3rd millennium BC. Length 46 cm.

105. Small handled jug, gold, Alacahöyük, second half of the 3rd millennium BC. Height 14.3 cm.

106. Bowl with studs on the shoulder, gold, Alacahöyük, second half of the 3rd millennium BC. Height 5.7 cm.

107. Handled cup, gold, Alacahöyük, second half of the 3rd millennium BC. Height 3.9 cm.

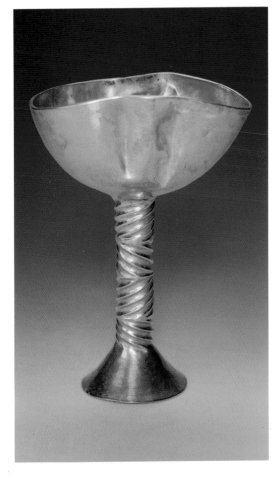

108. Cup, gold, Alacahöyük, second half of the 3rd millennium BC. Height 13.9 cm.

109. Cup, gold, Alacahöyük, second half of the 3rd millennium BC. Height 12.5 cm.

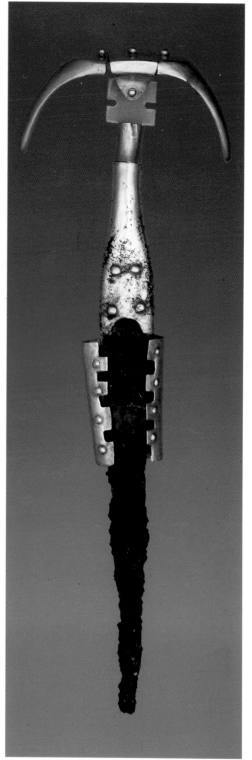

110. Pick-axe, bronze and gold, Alacahöyük, second half of the
3rd millennium BC. Length 15.2 cm.

111. Dagger with scabbard, gold and iron, Alacahöyük, second
half of the 3rd millennium BC. Length 18.5 cm.

112. Vessel decorated with a human face, terracotta, Karataş-Semayük, mid-3rd millennium BC.
Height 28 cm. Potters in western Anatolia continued an old tradition by using the image of the
Mother Goddess on vessels of various shapes. These pots are very widespread, and their origins
lie in the Neolithic and Chalcolithic Ages.

113. Vessel, terracotta, Alacahöyük, second half of the 3rd millennium BC. Height 23 cm.

115. Spouted jug, terracotta, stray find from the area around Ankara, beginning of the 3rd millennium BC. Height 20 cm.

114. Cruet of four bowls, terracotta, Beycesultan, beginning of the 3rd millennium BC. Height 7.5 cm.

117. Stylized female statuette (idol), silver, Alacahöyük,
second half of the 3rd millennium BC.
Height 7 cm.

116. Two-handled drinking cup (depas amphikypellon),
Karaoğlan, mid-3rd millennium BC.

118. Stylized female statuette (idol), terracotta,
Karaoğlan, second half of the
3rd millennium BC. Height 3.1 cm.

119. Stylized female statuette (idol), terracotta,
Etiyokuşu, mid-3rd millennium BC.
Height 6.4 cm.

120. Stylized female statuette (idol), terracotta, stray find from
Kalınkaya, end of the 3rd millennium BC. Height 9.3 cm.

121. Idols, alabaster,
Beycesultan and
Kültepe, begin-
ning of the 3rd
millennium BC.
Height 5.2 cm.

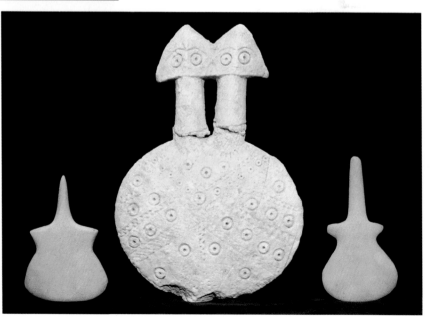

122. Views of the excavations at Kültepe.

THE ASSYRIAN COLONIES PERIOD

(1950 - 1750 B.C.)

The beginning of this period marks also the beginning of written history and the Middle Bronze Age in Anatolia. In 1960 B. C. the Old Assyrian State which was located in northern Mesopotamia established a sophisticated trading system with Anatolia. In this period Anatolia was split up into a number of feudal city states, mostly governed by Hattians. Since the Akkadian Period the Mesopotamians had known about the rich resources of Anatolia. Now, under the initiative of the Assyrians, they established systematic trading relations with their neighbours in the north. The Assyrian merchants introduced into Anatolia their language, the cuneiform script and the use of cylinder seals. In 1950 B.C. thus began written history in Anatolia. The merchants employed donkey caravans for their journeys to and from Anatolia. They used the Diyarbakır, Urfa, Maraş, Malatya road or the Adana - Taurus route (through the Cilician Gates). They imported tin, goat hair felt, cloth, garments, ornaments and perfumes from Assyria and exported goods made of silver and gold. From the Anatolian rulers they acquired rights of security for their markets and goods and for the roads. They paid tax and rent on their activities. They had no political or military aims. They established their markets in Anatolia outside the cities where the local rulers lived. They had nearly 20 markets called "Karums". The central market was established at the Karum of Kaniş, in the lower city of Kültepe. All the Karums in Anatolia came under the control of the Karum of Kaniş. The Karum of Kaniş was responsible to Assyria.

The merchants from Assyria who came to Anatolia to trade lived together with the local people in the Karums. Most of the tablets that have been unearthed in the excavation of the houses where Assyrian merchants lived are preserved in our Museum. They are written in the cuneiform script. Apart from Kültepe, other centres have also produced such written documents. These records were kept on rectangular clay tablets written with a specially shaped stylus using the cuneiform script in the language of Old Assyria. The tablets and their envelopes were fired together after the envelopes had been written and sealed. The tablets mostly concern trading activities, but there are also some recording the private and social lives of the merchants.

During the Colony Period pottery was

commonly produced on the potter's wheel, written history had begun and the Hittites appeared in Anatolia for the first time. The name of the king of Kaniş, Anitta, is known from a cuneiform inscription that was written on a bronze dagger. The dagger is among the finds from the Colony Period and is on display in our Museum. There are also various figurines of the fertility goddess, who was called Kubaba in the Hittite language, made from ivory, faience, lead and baked clay. The birth of Old Hittite art can be observed in these statuettes displayed in the Museum. The art of the Colony Period was generally a mixture of Hittite style with the traditions of Early Bronze Age and the influences of Hatti and Mesopotamia. This synthesis can be seen on the seals of the Colony Period unearthed at Kültepe, Acemhöyük, Alişar and Boğazköy. The cylinder seals and impressions produced in the Anatolian style and called the Anatolian group can be distinguished by their figural representations.

The art of this period is represented in the Museum by seals, small statuettes, mould - made lead figurines of gods and the gods' families and libation vessels (bibru). When the dress styles, weapons and helmets of the gods on the lead figurines are compared with Hittite deities, it is seen that the shapes of the helmets, horns, weapons, belts and short skirts are features known from the antelopes, pigs, eagles, cats, sharply pointed boots and snails. In addition, we have in our Museum beak - spouted jugs, teapots and fruit bowls with multiple handles. The shapes of these cups were taken from the Early Bronze Age but with their very glossy, metallic appearance they are the most beautiful examples of this period. The painted pottery of the period is characterized by black, brown or red geometric patterns on cream surfaces.

Kültepe (Kaniş with its Karum), Acemhöyük, Alişar and Boğazköy are the principal Anatolian centres of the Colony Age. It is from these sites that the finds on display in our Museum come. There are very close similarities between these centres in the fields of city planning, architecture and small finds. The small finds, made of precious materials and found in graves or houses, represent the art of the period: gold objects and ornaments, bronze tools, figurines and vases made of ivory, obsidian and rock crystal. Ivory makes its first appearance in Anatolian archaeology during this period. The ivory objects from the excavations at Acemhöyük and Kültepe are good examples on their kind.

In addition, there are also displayed in the Museum seal impressions (bullae) and cuneiform documents that shed light on the history of the countries that were the neighbours of Anatolia in the Colony Period.

123. View of the store room containing large pithoi (storage jars), excavated at Kültepe.

124. View of the excavations at Kültepe.

125. Artist's impression of Kültepe, showing the compound (Karum) used by Assyrian merchants for their mule trains, situated below the fortified city of Prince Kaniş. The building on the right is the headquarters of this trade organization, while behind it at top right is part of the volcanic mountain now known as Erciyes Dağı.

126. An unopened clay envelope, Kültepe, 19th century BC. Height 11.1 cm.

127. Cylinder seal, serpentine, Kültepe, first quarter of the 2nd millennium BC. Height 2.5 cm.

128. Clay tablet and envelope, Kültepe, 19th century BC. Height 16.2 cm.

130. Strainer vessel, terracotta, Kültepe,
19th century BC. Height 14.5 cm.

129. Ritual vessel with human face in relief, terracotta,
Kültepe, 19th century BC. Height 15.5 cm. Vessels
with a tall foot come in a wide variety of shapes and can
be monochrome or decorated with a painted design.
This example, with its face relief and horn-shaped handle, represents a continuation in the second millennium
BC of the Early Bronze Age tradition of decorating pottery with human faces.

131. Vessel with trefoil rim, terracotta, Kültepe,
19th century BC. Height 32.5 cm.

132. Beak-spouted jug, terracotta,
     Kültepe, 19th century BC.
     Height 16.2 cm.

133. Beak-spouted jug, terracotta,
     Kültepe, 19th century BC.
     Height 19.2 cm.

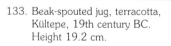

134. Beak-spouted jug, terracotta,
     Kültepe, 19th century BC.
     Height 16 cm.

135. Spouted and lidded jug, terracotta, Kültepe,
18th century BC. Height 29.5 cm.

136. Beak-spouted jug, terracotta, Kültepe,
18th century BC. Height 44 cm.

137. Spouted jug, terracotta, Kültepe,
18th century BC. Height 20 cm.

138. Vessel with relief decoration, terracotta, Kültepe,
18th century BC. Height 42 cm.

139. Bowl with tall base, terracotta, Kültepe,
19th century BC. Height 21.7 cm.

140. Squat spouted vessel, terracotta, Kültepe,
18th century BC. Height 16 cm.

141. Vessel with tall base, terracotta, Kültepe, 18th century BC. Height 27.5 cm.

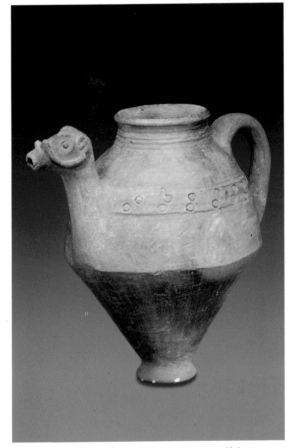

142. Jug with animal-headed spout, terracotta, Kültepe, 18th century BC. Height 23 cm.

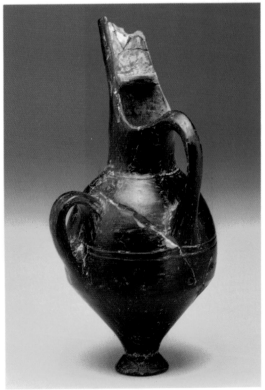

143. Beak-spouted jug, terracotta, Kültepe, 18th century BC. Height 26 cm.

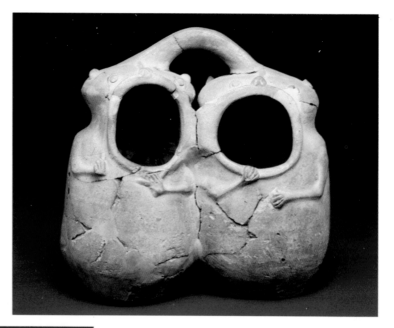

144. Vessel with two compart-
ments in the shape of human
figures, terracotta, Kültepe,
19th century BC.
Height 31.5 cm.

145. Vase with relief decoration of bulls' heads, terracotta, Kültepe, 18th century BC. Height 62 cm.

146. One-handled beaker, terracotta, Kültepe,
18th century BC. Height 9.3 cm.

147. Ritual vessel in the shape of a boat, terracotta, Kültepe, 19th century BC. Length 24 cm.

148. Ritual vessel in the shape of a boat, terracotta, Kültepe, 19th century BC. Length 18.8 cm.

149. Ritual vessel in the shape of a boat, terracotta, Kültepe, 19th century BC. Length 24 cm.

150. Spouted jug on a tripod stand, terracotta, Kültepe, 19th century BC. Height (jug) 12.4 cm, (stand) 17 cm. The use of the potter's wheel became widespread during this period, which led to a great increase in the variety of vessel shapes. Some of these vessels were stamped with seal impressions.

151. Vase on a tall pedestal (fruit bowl), terracotta, Kültepe, 19th century BC. Height 42.5 cm.

152. Bath tub, terracotta, Kültepe, 18th century BC. Height 86 cm. The tub is hand-made with a burnished surface. Inside there is a seat with two drainage holes in it.

153. Boar-shaped ritual drinking vessel, terracotta, Kültepe, 19th century BC. Height 14.8 cm.

154. Lion-shaped ritual drinking vessel in the shape of a lion, terracotta, Kültepe, 19th century BC. Height 12.5 cm.

155. Boar-shaped ritual drinking vessel, terracotta, Kültepe, 19th century BC.

156. Boar-shaped ritual drinking vessel, terracotta, Kültepe, 19th century BC. Height 8.5 cm.

157. Lion-shaped ritual drinking vessel, terracotta, Kültepe, 19th century BC. Height 19.5 cm.

158. Dog-shaped ritual drinking vessel, terracotta, Kültepe, 19th century BC. Height 9 cm.

159. Deer-shaped ritual drinking vessel, terracotta,
Kültepe, 19th century BC. Height 19 cm.

160. Eagle-shaped ritual drinking vessel, terracotta,
Kültepe, 19th century BC. Height 15.5 cm.

161. Eagle-shaped ritual
drinking vessel, terra-
cotta, Kültepe,
19th century BC.
Height 12.5 cm.

162. Rabbit-shaped ritual drinking vessel, terracotta, Kültepe, 19th century BC. Height 10.5 cm.

163. Sandal-shaped ritual drinking vessel, terracotta, Kültepe, 19th century BC. Height 8.2 cm.

164. Ritual drinking vessel, terracotta, Kültepe, 19th century BC. Height 6.4 cm.

165. Eagle-shaped ritual drinking vessel, terracotta, Kültepe, 19th century BC. Height 20.7 cm.

166. Spouted, two-handled vessel, terracotta, Acemhöyük, 19th century BC. Height 16 cm.

167. Ritual drinking vessel in the shape of an eagle's head, terracotta, Kültepe, 19th century BC. Height 13.1 cm.

168. Dish and saucer, stone, Acemhöyük, 18th century BC. Height 6.5 cm.

169. Ritual drinking vessel, terracotta, Kültepe, 19th century BC. Height 15.6 cm.

111

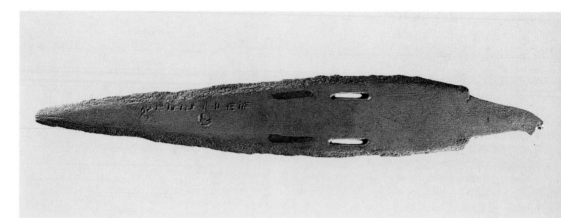

170. Dagger belonging to King Anitta, bronze, Kültepe, 18th century BC. Length 29 cm.

171. Spool, bronze, Kültepe, 18th century BC.
Height 10.8 cm.

172. Spool, bronze, Kültepe, 18th century BC.
Height 8.8 cm.

173. Figurine of a god, lead, Kültepe, 18th century BC. Height 6.5 cm.

175. Statuette of a naked woman, ivory, Kültepe, 18th century BC. Height 9.3 cm.

174. Mould for figurines, steatite, Kültepe, 18th century BC. Height 6.2 cm.

176. Vase, rock crystal, Acemhöyük, 19th century BC. Height 16.3 cm.

178. Drinking vessel in the shape of fruit bowl with a bull-headed spout, terracotta, Kültepe, 19th century BC. Height 46 cm.

177. Fragment of a vessel, obsidian, Acemhöyük, 19th century BC. Height 16.7 cm.

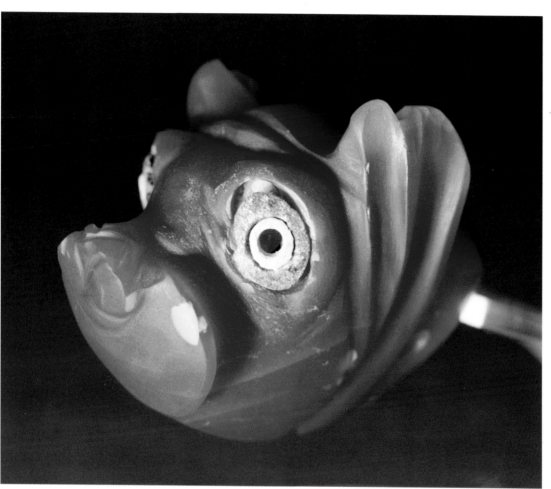

179. Boar's head, agate, Kültepe, 18th century BC. Height 4.1 cm.

180. Stamp seal, gold, Kültepe,
18th century BC. Diameter 1 cm.

181. Boğazköy. The Lion's Gate, Large Citadel, Upper City.

182. Boğazköy. View of the Large Temple, Lower City.

OLD HITTITE AND HITTITE IMPERIAL PERIODS

(1750 - 1200 B.C.)

According to written records, Anitta, the son of Pithana, established the Hittite kingdom in the last phases of the Colony Age by uniting the Hittites then living in different city - states.

The capital of the state was moved from Neşa (Kaniş) to Hattuşa (Boğazköy) by Hattuşili I after the disappearance of the Assyrian trading colonies from Anatolia. This period is known as the Old Hittite period. The finds unearthed from the excavations at Alacahöyük, Eskiyapar, İnandık and Maşathöyük reveal that the art of the period remained faithful to the traditions of the Anatolian style. The pottery in the Hittite period, continued with only minor alterations the same shapes and techniques that had existed during the Assyrian colony period. The popular ritual - cups were produced in somewhat larger dimensions, as for example, the bulls' head rhyta found at Boğazköy and İnandık.

The tradition of making relief - decorated vases, which is known from the Colony Age continued; the best examples have been discovered at Eskiyapar, İnandık and Bitik. Before the excavation of these sites relief - decorated vases of this age had not been found. The İnandık Vase, which was decorated with relief motifs in friezes, is the finest example of this type. The common pottery shapes of the period were large bowls for washing, vessels in the shape of flasks, kantharos, vessels with strainers and cult vessels in the form of goddesses.

One of two examples representing the state of metallurgy in this period comes from Boğazköy. It is a gold necklace in the shape of a seated goddess. The other is a bronze figurine of a deity from Dövlek. The bronze statuettes of Old Hittite figural art represent gods. It is known from written records that these figurines, which were thought to have protective powers, were kept in the temples.

The Old Hittite Kingdom's power was diminished for a time because of domestic power struggles, but during the second half of the 2nd millennium B.C., in the time of Suppiluliuma I, they regained their dominance and created an empire, that became one of the three most powerful states in the Near East, the others being Egypt and Babylon.

Examples of Hittite art, which reached a very advanced level in the Hittite Imperial Period, have been unearthed not only at sites in the Hittite homeland but also in all the Near Eastern cities which came under the domination of the Hittites or which felt the effects of Hittite political influence. The finds from the capital Hattuşa / Boğazköy, Alacahöyük, Eskiyapar and from all the other sites throughout Anatolia that were under the Hittite control constitute the most important collection of objects representing Hittite art. That these objects are fine examples of Hittite art is confirmed by the results of stratigraphic excavations, by stylistic similarities and by descriptions found in the written records of the Hittite period.

The emergence of Hittite Imperial art can be dated to about 1400 B.C. and continued without interruption until Hittite political power collapsed in 1200 B. C. During this period the finest examples of Hittite art were produced.

Hittite representational art describes the religious and historical events relating to the Kingdom between the time of Assyrian trading colonies and 1200 B.C. Events relating to everyday life also included religious functions since the sources of Hittite art were mainly religious and royal.

The plans and the construction techniques of the Hittite sanctuaries at Boğazköy display common characteristics. There are rooms and porticos around an enclosed courtyard. The statues of the gods were kept in sacred inner rooms called cella. These Hittite sanctuaries formed the nucleus of grand establishments with a large number of staff. There are several gates in the city wall decorated with reliefs of deities, sphinxes and lions. For example, there is the relief of the War God at the King's Gate. The War God is worked in such high relief that it has the appearance of a statue, it is claimed in the Hittite records that statues of even larger proportions were also made in this period.

Another group of finds which are evidence of representational art in the Hittite Imperial Period are the stone orthostats (a row of upright blocks in the foot of a wall). The finest examples of stones used for architectural purposes are the Alacahöyük orthostats. Groups of decorated orthostats have not been found at any other centre apart from Alacahöyük. Religious subjects, such as can be seen on other examples of Hittite art, are depicted on these orthostats. The orthostats are on display in the central hall of the Museum.

In addition to over life - sized statues and orthostats, there are miniature figurines of deities made of gold, ivory, bronze and stone and small reliefs made in the same style. On these objects the gods are represented with large almond - shaped eyes, joined eyebrows, large (Roman) noses and smiling lips. On the reliefs the heads and feet are shown in profile whereas the bodies are shown frontally. These are all Hittite characteristics.

The tradition of the Old Hittite stamp seals continued into this period. In addition to stamp seals, ring seals and bullas came into use. There was, however, considerable development in the shapes of the seals and in the figural scenes. On these seals hieroglyphic writing was used together with cuneiform script, making them easy to read.

In the Imperial Period there is a decrease in the number of cup shapes and a regression in technology. Only vessels which have religious significance were carefully produced. The vessels in the shape of an animal, representing the two bulls of the Storm God, and the vessel representing the sacred precinct are parficularly important.

One of the written records found at Boğazköy concerns the Treaty of Kadeş ca. 1270 BC. It was signed after the Battle of Kadeş between the Hittites and Egyptians. It is the first written treaty known in Anatolia. The original of the agreement was cut on a silver tablet but duplicates were made on baked clay. These clay tablets are, however, are amongst the most important archival material. Another important document is a bronze tablet found at Boğazköy in 1986. This tablet is written in cuneiform script. It measures 23.5 x 34.5 cm and deals with arrangements concerning the frontiers of the Hittite Empire. This is the first bronze tablet to be found in Anatolia.

183. Bull's head-shaped ritual drinking cup, terracotta, Kültepe, 18th-17th century BC. Height 14.5 cm.

184. Bull's head-shaped ritual drinking cup, terracotta, Kültepe, 18th-17th century BC. Height 14.5 cm.

185. Ritual drinking vessel, terracotta, Beycesultan, 18th-17th century BC. Height 13.1 cm.

187. Ritual drinking vessels, terracotta, Alişar, 17th-16th century BC. Height 8.9 cm.

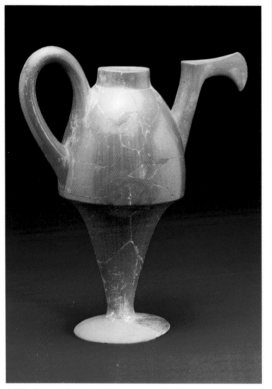

186. Spouted vessel with tall foot, terracotta, Alacahöyük, 17th-16th century BC. Height 32 cm.

188. Bull's head-shaped ritual drinking cup, terracotta, Alacahöyük, 17th-16th century BC. Height 7.7 cm.

189. Bull-shaped ritual vessel, terracotta, Inandık,
17th-16th century BC. Height 31.4 cm.

191. Beak-spouted jug, terracotta, Inandık,
17th-16th century BC. Height 51 cm.

190. Deity seated in an alcove, terracotta, Inandık,
17th-16th century BC. Height 16.3 cm.

122

192. Relief vase, terracotta, İnandık, mid-17th century BC. Height 82 cm.

193. Strainer, terracotta, Inandık,
17th century BC. Height 22.7 cm.

194. Drinking cup (kantharos), terracotta, Inandık,
17th century BC. Height 33.4 cm.

195. One-handled vessel containing figures participating in a ritual, terracotta,
Eskiyapar, 17th-16th century BC. Height 8.4 cm.

196. Pilgrim flask (water bottle), terracotta, Eskiyapar, 18th century BC. Height 42 cm.

198. Vessel decorated with rams' heads in relief, terracotta, Eskiyapar, 18th century BC. Height 12.3 cm.

197. Spouted pouring jug, terracotta, Eskiyapar, 18th century BC. Height 15.8 cm.

199. One-handled vessel, terracotta, Eskiyapar,
18th century BC. Height 29 cm.

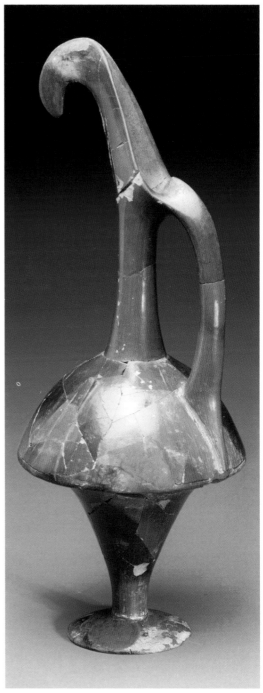

200. Beak-spouted jug, terracotta, Eskiyapar,
18th century BC. Height 45 cm.

201. Vessel in the shape of a two-headed duck, terracota, Boğazköy, 14th century BC. Height 20.2 cm.

203. Ritual vessel in the shape of a tower, terracotta, Boğazköy, 18th century BC. Height 32.5 cm.

202. Beak-spouted jug, terracotta, Boğazköy, 17th - 16th century BC. Height 135 cm.

204. Bull-shaped vessels, terracotta, Boğazköy, 16th century BC. Height 90 cm. These objects show the care that was taken in the making of pottery for religious uses, especially ritual drinking cups. These two vessels, in the shape of bulls symbolizing the Storm God, are unique.

205. Pilgrim flask (water bottle), terracotta, Eskiyapar, 2nd millennium BC. Height 49 cm.

207. Vessel rim shaped like a tower, terracotta, Boğazköy, 14th century BC. Height 12 cm.

206. Ring-shaped vessel, terracotta, Boğazköy, 16th century BC. Height 30 cm.

208. Vessel in the
     shape of a
     bunch of
     grapes, terra-
     cotta,
     Boğazköy, 18th
     century BC.
     Height 14 cm.

209. Bull's head, terracotta, Tokat, 17th-16th century BC. Height (chin to top of head) 15.8 cm.

210. Clay tablet,
Boğazköy,
13th century BC.
Height 9.9 cm.
The text is a letter of
friendship from
Naptera, wife of
King Ramses II of
Egypt, to Puduhepa,
wife of the Hittite
king, Hattushili III.

211. Seal impression of
King Urhi-Teshup,
terracotta,
Boğazköy,
13th century BC.
Height 3.9 cm.

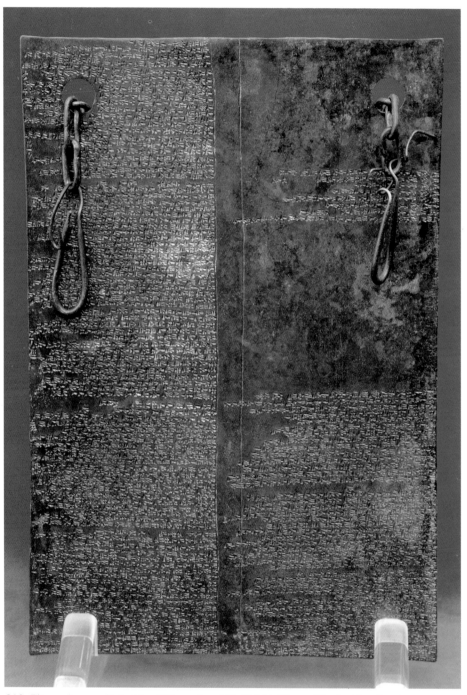

212. Plaque, bronze, Boğazköy, 13th century BC. Height 35 cm. The text is a border agreement between the Hittite king, Tuthaliya IV, and Kurunta, King of Tarhuntassha.

213. Seal ring, gold, Alacahöyük, 14th-13th century BC. Diameter 1.9 cm.

214. Vessel with hieroglyph inscription, silver, unprovenanced,
second half of the 2nd millennium BC. Height 7.3 cm.

215. Statuette of a god, bronze, Dövlek near Şarkışla, Sivas (stray find), 16th-15th century BC. Height 11.4 cm. The Hittites commonly made small statues and reliefs for religious purposes. This example represents a young, athletic deity striding forward, with his arms in a pose suggesting that he is hurling a missile.

217. Pendant in the shape of a seated goddess, gold,
Boğazköy, 15th century BC. Height 2 cm.

216. Statuette of a god, silver and gold, unprovenanced,
15th-14th century BC. Height 4.4 cm.

218. Statuette of the Sun Goddess, bronze,
Alacahöyük, 14th-13th century BC.
Height 11 cm.

219. Statuette of a seated man, ivory, Alacahöyük,
14th-13th century BC. Height 3.9 cm.

221. Relief of a god, steatite, Yeniköy near Çorum,
14th - 13th century BC. Height 6.4 cm.

220. Statuette of the God Bes, bone, Alacahöyük,
14th - 13th century BC. Height 4.9 cm.

137

222. Statuette of a mountain god, ivory, Boğazköy, 14th century BC. Height 3.6 cm.

223. Relief of a warrior god, limestone, Boğazköy, 14th-13th century BC. Height 225 cm. The relief comes from the inner face of the left side of the King's Gate in the city walls. It represents the figure of a so-called warrior god, carved in such high relief that it appears almost to be a three-dimensional statue.

224. Relief depicting a figure in a long robe (perhaps a priest) leading a flock of sheep, andesite, Alacahöyük, 14th century BC. Height 133 cm.

226. Relief depicting acrobats, andesite, Alacahöyük, 14th century BC. Height 116 cm.

225. Relief depicting a king and queen praying in front of an altar on which stands the figure of a bull, andesite, Alacahöyük, 14th century BC. Height 126 cm.

227. Relief depicting three figures in long robe (perhaps priests), andesite, Alacahöyük, 14th century BC. Height 133 cm. Such a series of reliefs (orthostats) has not been found at any other Hittite site. At Alacahöyük they stood flanking either side of the Sphinx Gate and clearly depict scenes associated with religious ceremonies.

228. Aerial view of the excavations at Aslantepe near Malatya.

229. Neo-Hittite relief of King Warpalawas, stone, Andaval near Niğde, 9th century BC. Diameter 36 cm. The inscription accompanying the relief contains the name of a city called Na-hi-ta, which may be identified with modern Niğde.

THE NEO - HITTITE STATES

(1200 - 700 B.C.)

The Hittite Empire came to an end around 1200 B.C. as a result of disruptions caused by the invasion of the so - called Sea Peoples. The Hittites who survived these invasions moved to the south and south east of the Taurus mountains and settled there. They were known as the Neo - Hittites. After this event they were unable to re - establish a centralized Hittite state, but Hittite traditions were continued by the rulers until 700 B.C., the year in which, after repeated attack by the Assyrians they completely disappeared from history.

In excavations carried out at Carchemish, Zincirli, Malatya - Aslantepe, Sakçagözü, Karatepe and Tell Tayinat, important centres of the Neo - Hittite period have been discovered. Finds belonging to this culture have also been found at numerous other sites. These small city - states coexisted with the other political powers of the first quarter of the 1st millennium B. C.: the Phrygian Kingdom in northern and western Anatolia, the Urartian Kingdom in eastern Anatolia and the Assyrian Empire in northern Mesopotamia.

The Neo - Hittite cities were surrounded by defensive walls. The administrative and religious monumental buildings, placed on the highest point on each site, formed the citadel and the main protected area of the city. This was surrounded by additional defensive walls. The cities were planned as a single unit consisting of palaces, streets, monumental stairs and squares. The palaces were usually large complexes built around a courtyard. These structures, which were called "Hilani", were architectural features peculiar to the period. They were rectangular structures with columns at the entrances.

Another important characteristic of Neo - Hittite art was the incorporation of sculpture in architectural settings. The gates in the city walls and the facades of the palaces were covered with relief - decorated stone blocks (orthostats).

The region that they occupied lay on the trade routes to the Near East on the one side and to the Aegean Coast through the Central Anatolia on the other. Hence the influences of the Hittites and the Hurri - Mitannians, who arrived in this region in the second half of the 2nd millennium B.C., and of the Aramaians, who settled in the same region during the 1st millennium B. C., are clearly seen on the regional art forms.

In the Museum of Anatolian Civilizations, Neo - Hittite Art is represented by sculpture. The reliefs found on the city - gate of the Aslantepe near Malatya and the two lion statues form a group reflecting traditional Hittite features. On these reliefs there is a representation of Sulumeli, King of the Malatya region, presenting drinks to gods and goddesses. The statue of a Great King found at the entrance of the Aslantepe palace displays Assyrian features and is, therefore, dated to later period.

The most important city kingdom of the Neo - Hittites was Carchemisch in south - eastern Anatolia. Its importance was due to its location on the crossroads from Mesopotamia and Egypt to Central Anatolia. Most of the finds in the Museum are from Carchemish: the reliefs of Uzunduvar (long wall), Kral Burcu (King's tower), Kahramanlar Duvarı (wall of the Hero's) and Su Kapısı (Water Gate) are on display in the Museum in their original positions. On the reliefs various scenes are depicted: the religious ceremonies held for the Goddess Kubaba; the appointment of Kamanas, who was the eldest son of Arasas, the King of Carchemisch, as the heir apparent; the war chariots and victory scenes from the war with the Assyrians; and the gods and goddesses and various creatures of Hittite mythology. Both Hittite and Assyrian features are to be observed on the reliefs.

On the Sakçagözü reliefs, however, found at the entrance of the palace, Assyrian and Aramaian influences are very strong. They are, therefore, dated to the end of the 8th century B.C.

On the Malatya, Sakçagözü and Carchemish reliefs there are depictions of the Moon God. One of these shows the Moon God with wings on his head, and on another the winged Moon God is wearing a hat with a crescent on it. These reliefs indicate that the worship of the Sun and Moon Gods continued to be practised during this period.

Another common feature of the Neo - Hittite city - states was Hittite hieroglyphic writing. During this period the cuneiform script was no longer used. Its place had been taken by the Hittite hieroglyphs, which can be seen on such monuments as the Andaval relief and on the Sultanı - Kayseri and Köylüotu stelae, as well as on the Carchemish reliefs.

The Neo - Hittite Period is important in the archaeology and art of Anatolia as evidence for the survival of the Hittites until 700 B. C.

230. Statue of King Tarhunza, limestone, Aslantepe near Malatya, 8th century BC. Height 318 cm. Details of the figure's appearance and costume show a strong Assyrian influence; note especially his wavy hair and beard, the diadem and the knotted sandals.

231. Relief depicting King Sulumeli offering a libation to a god, basalt, Aslantepe near Malatya, 10th-9th century BC. Height 86.2 cm.

232. Relief depicting a lion hunt, basalt, Aslantepe near Malatya, 9th-8th century BC. Height 53.4 cm.

233. Relief depicting a banquet, sandstone, stray find, Malatya, 10th-9th century BC. Height 52 cm.

234. Gate lion, limestone, Aslantepe near Malatya, 10th-9th century BC. Height 124 cm.

235 - A. Neo-Hittite hieroglyphic inscription, basalt, Carchemish, second half of the 8th century BC. Height 111 cm.

235 - B. Relief depicting King Araras with his so Kamanas, basalt, Carchemish, secon half of the 8th century BC. Height 114.6 cm.

237. Relief of helmeted soldiers, basalt, Carchemish, second half of the 8th century BC. Height 133 cm.

36 - A. Relief depicting the children of King Araras, basalt, Carchemish, second half of the 8th century BC. Height 119 cm.

236 - B. Relief depicting the wife of King Araras, holding their youngest child in her arms and leading a goat, basalt, Carchemish, second half of the 8th century BC. Height 115.2 cm.

38. Relief of palace officials, basalt, Carchemish, second half of the 8th century BC. Height 111 cm.

239. Relief fragment with bust of the Goddess Kubaba, basalt, Carchemish, 9th century BC. Height 82 cm. The figure, made in a traditional style, is identified as Kubaba by the horn on her forehead and the pomegranate she holds.

240. Reliefs depicting the Goddess Kubaba seated on a throne supported by recumbent lions and a procession of women, basalt, Carchemish, 9th century BC. Height 90 and 112 cm.

241. Reliefs of men carrying animals to a sacrifice, basalt, Carchemish, 9th century BC. Height 100 cm.

242. Relief of a war chariot, basalt, Carchemish, 8th century BC. Height 175 cm.
The figures imitate a typical Assyrian scene.

152

243. Relief of a sphinx with human and lion heads, basalt, Carchemish, 9th century BC. Height 113 cm. A very well-preserved example of the orthostats found at Carchemish. The nose of the human head indicates a Luvian or Hittite origin.

244. Relief of King Katuvas with a long hieroglyphic inscription, basalt, Carchemish, 9th century BC. Height 128 cm.

245. Neo-Hittite hieroglyphic inscription, basalt, Carchemish, 9th century BC. Height 136 cm.

246. Pair of sphinxes, basalt, Sakçagözü, 8th century BC. Height 85 cm.

247A. Relief depicting gods sanctifying the Tree of Life under a Winged Sun Disk, basalt, Sakçagözü, second half of the 8th century BC. Height 86.3 cm.

247B. Relief of a winged mythical creature with the head of a bird and the body of a man, basalt, Sakçagözü, second half of the 8th century BC. Height 86 cm.

247C. Gate lion, basalt, Sakçagözü, second half of the 8th century BC. Height 84 cm.

248. Relief of mythical creatures, some with the head of a man and the body of a bull, others with the head of a lion and the body of a man, basalt, Carchemish, 9th century BC. Height 117 cm.

249. Relief of a heroic figure overcoming wild animals, basalt, Carchemish, 9th century BC. Height 117 cm.

250. Lion hunt, basalt, Carchemish, 9th century BC. Height 130 cm.

251. Relief of two bird-men, basalt, Carchemish, 9th century BC. Height 125 cm

252. Gordion, the Phrygian capital, is surrounded by tumuli (burial mounds) of various sizes. The largest is the Great Tumulus, measuring nearly 300 m. in diameter and 50 m. in height. Not only in terms of size but also in the construction of the wooden burial chamber and the grave goods, this monumental tomb is without parallel.

253. Reconstruction of the wooden burial chamber of King Midas, Gordion, 8th century BC.

PHRYGIANS

(1200 - 700 B.C.)

At the beginning of the 12th century B.C., the Phrygians arrived in Anatolia from south - east Europe in the wake of the Aegean migrations. They laid waste all the important centres and brought - about the fall of the Hittite Empire. Then, gradually, they took over control of Anatolia. However, the main area that the Phrygians settled was the Sakarya valley which is bounded by the Afyon, Kütahya and Eskişehir regions. Gordion was their capital. The few surviving inscriptions of the Phrygians show that their language was Indo - European. The Greek sources, especially Herodotus, state that the Phrygians came from Mecedonia where they were known as Greater and Lesser Byriges, while the Assyrian sources mention the Mita, King of the Mushki. It is now accepted that Mita and Midas are identical and the Mushki of the Assyrian sources are the Phrygians.

In the second half of the 8th century B.C. the Phrygian Kingdom became very powerful but, after the invasion of the Cimmerians at the beginning of the 7th century B.C., their power declined. A short time after this event they came under the control of the Kingdom of Lydia. In 550 B. C. they fell to the Persians and lost their freedom completely.

The political life and art of the Phrygians developed in two stages: the Early (the period before the 7th century B.C.) and the Late (the period from the Cimmerian invasions in 695 B.C. until the last quarter of the 4th century B.C.). We know very little about Phrygian art in the early part of the first period, and most of our knowledge comes from the time after 750 B.C.

Gordion, the capital of Phrygia, was a fortified city surrounded by strong defensive walls. The public or official buildings of the city were constructed in the so - called megaron plan - rectangular buildings built in stone, mud - brick and wood - a technique which had been known in Anatolia since the 3rd millennium B.C. The Phrygians decorated the roofs of their buildings with geometric - patterned terracotta panels in the traditional style of Western Anatolia and covered the floors with polychrome mosaics. The finest examples of these painted terracotta panels in our Museum come from Gordion and Pazarlı. On these panels warriors, lion and bull fights, figures of creatures with human or bird heads and horse bodies, and goats on each side of the tree - of - life were depicted.

Apart from Gordion on the banks of the Sakarya river, sites in the bend and on the south of the Kızılırmak river such as Alacahöyük, Boğazköy, Pazarlı, Kültepe, Eskiyapar and Maşathöyük provide a good source of information for the Phrygians and their art. The rock monuments of Phrygia and the objects unearthed on other settlements show that Phrygian architecture had deep rooted traditions.

The families of the Phrygian Kings and the nobles were buried in built chambers made of juniper and cedar timbers and covered with a high mound of soil known as a tumulus. The wooden construction of these tomb - chambers show an advanced level of which wooden chambers were then built, and the space surrounding the chambers was filled with rubble. The roof was built after the dead body and the gifts had been placed in the wooden chamber. A large pile of stones was heaped over this roof and then covered with soil or clay to form the tumulus. Twentyfive of the nearly one hundred known Phrygian tumuli have been excavated. The richness and the variety of the grave gifts demonstrates the status of the buried person.

Apart from Gordion, important Phrygian tumuli have been discovered in interior - west central Anatolia, around Afyon and Eskişehir, and also near Ankara. Those in Ankara are sit-uated in the Anıtkabir and Atatürk Farm districts. The tumuli belong to the periods between 8th and 7th centuries B.C. Their height differs between 3 metres and 40 metres. In the earlier periods dead bodies were buried directly in ground whereas in the later periods there was a tradition of cremation, the ashes being placed in special vases and then left under tumuli. The largest Phrygian tumulus is at Gordion. It reaches a height of 50m and has a diameter of 300 m. The size of the wooden inner chamber is 6.20 m by 5.15 m. The room has a triangular pediment but has no door. The skeleton of a person 1.59 m in height and more than 60 years old was found on a large wooden couch in one corner of the chamber. This monumental tomb is thought to belong to King Midas. In it were found some large bronze cauldrons full of small vessels; they are set on bronze tripods next to wooden panels decorated in relief with geometric motifs. The small vessels in the cauldrons include omphalos bowls, bowls with swivel handles, buckets, small cauldrons and ladles, together with a large number of bronze fibulae. The Phrygians developed an individual style in making of cauldrons. They added their own concepts to those which were imported from the Urartians living in eastern Anatolia during the same period. The latter people attained a high level of metal - working technology, notably on the rims of cauldrons. The Phrygians used human heads fashioned in the Assyrian style whereas the Urartians used bulls' and lions' heads. The high level of workmanship seen in the geometric motifs that were made by engraving or inlaying techniques demonstrates that the Phrygians also attained a high level of technology in woodwork as well as metallurgy. The excavation of the tumuli has produced unique examples of Phrygians furniture decorated with geometric patterns, small figures of horses, small statues of bulls and lions fighting, and wooden relief panels showing mythological scenes. The Phrygians also produced ivory figures in their own distinctive style.

The individual style of the Phrygians is also to be seen in the "Cybele" figurines and reliefs and in the Cybele cult. Cybele, the chief goddess of the Phrygians, is to be identified with Kubaba of the Hittite pantheon in the 2nd millennium B.C. As a mother goddess she was the symbol of fertility and is usually represented with lions. The cult was introduced by the Phrygians to the Hellenistic and Roman world via Sardis. The "Cybele" figurines and reliefs in the Museum come from Boğazköy, Ankara and Gordion.

Another group of finds on display in the Museum are the andesite (a local Ankara stone) reliefs found in the Ankara region. On these reliefs the influence of Neo - Hittite and Assyrian styles can be detected. There are lions, horses, bulls, griffons and sphinxes on these orthostat blocks. These examples demonstrate the influence of Western Anatolian, Late Assyrian and Late Hittite styles on Phrygian art.

Phrygian wheel - made pottery is divided into two groups: the monochrome pottery and the decorated, polychrome pottery. The black or grey monochrome pottery produced in imitation of metal vessels is very common. On the decorated wares the patterns are usually reddish brown on a light - coloured surface. The motifs are usually rectangular, triangular, wavy or zig - zag lines, concentric circles and chequerboard patterns. Some of the wares were completely decorated with geometric patters. On some the patterns were divided into panels, decorated with animal motifs. Zoomorphic rhytons, reflecting the imagination and creativeness of the Phrygian artists, are a form of drinking vessel that had been in use in Anatolia since prehistoric times.

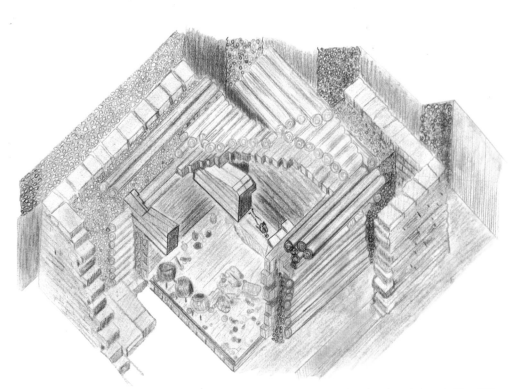

254. Artist's impression of the wooden burial chamber inside the Great Tumulus, thought to belong to King Midas.

255. Carved and inlaid stand or table, wood, Tumulus P at Gordion, 8th century BC. Height 30 cm.

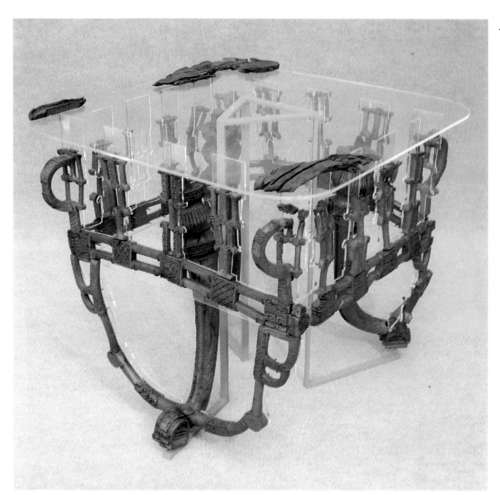

256. Inlaid table, wood, the Great Tumulus at Gordion, end of the 8th century BC. Height 64 cm.

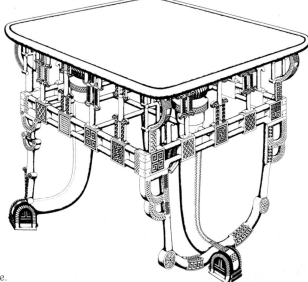

257. Reconstruction drawing of the table.

258. Serving table, wood, the Great Tumulus at Gordion, end of the 8th century BC. Height 94 cm.

259. Serving table, wood, the Great Tumulus at Gordion, end of the 8th century BC. Height 94 cm.

260. Reconstruction drawing of the table.

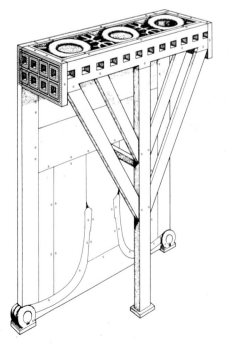

261. Lion-shaped child's toy, wood, Tumulus P at Gordion, end of the 8th - beginning of the 7th century BC. Height 7.5 cm.

262. Toys in the form of a lion and bull, wood, Tumulus P at Gordion, end of the 8th - beginning of the 7th century BC. Height 6.8 cm.

263. Toy in the form of a griffin eating a fish, wood, Tumulus P at Gordion, end of the 8th - beginning of the 7th century BC. Height 6.6 cm.

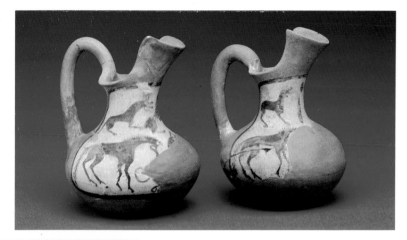

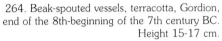

264. Beak-spouted vessels, terracotta, Gordion,
end of the 8th-beginning of the 7th century BC.
Height 15-17 cm.

265. Mug, terracotta, Alişar, 8th century BC.
Height 14 cm.

266. Long-spouted pouring vessel, terracotta,
Tumulus W at Gordion,
beginning of the 8th century BC.
Height 8 cm.

267. Jug with painted decoration, terracotta, Tumulus P at Gordion, end of the 8th - beginning of the 7th century BC. Height 30 cm. The tomb belongs to a child from the royal family.

268. Ritual drinking vessel in the shape of a goose, terracotta, Tumulus P at Gordion, end of the 8th-beginning of the 7th century BC. Height 37 cm.

269. Goat-shaped drinking vessel, terracotta, Tumulus P at Gordion,
end of the 8th-beginning of the 7th century BC.
Height 16 cm.

271. Painted vessel, terracotta, Tumulus P at Gordion,
end of the 8th-beginning of the 7th century BC.
Height 19.5 cm.

270. Goat-shaped drinking vessel, terracotta, Tumulus P at
Gordion,
end of the 8th-beginning of the 7th century BC.
Height 20.7 cm.

272. Ritual drinking vessel, terracotta, Gordion, end of the 8th-beginning of the 7th century BC. Height 25 cm.

273. Ritual drinking vessel, terracotta, Gordion, end of the 8th-beginning of the 7th century BC. Height 21.4 cm.

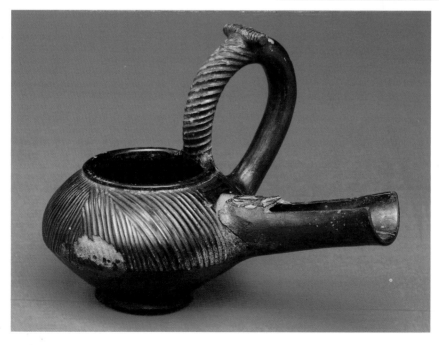

274. Mug with feeding
274. nozzle, terracotta, Gordion, end of the 8th-beginning of the 7th century BC. Height 12.1 cm.

277. Large painted vessel, terracotta, Kültepe, 6th century BC. Height 78 cm.

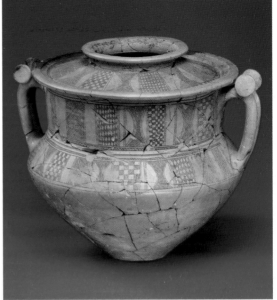

275. Painted vessel with trefoil mouth, terracotta, Gordion, 9th century BC. Height 21.5 cm.

276. Mixing bowl (krater), terracotta, Gordion, 9th century BC. Height 33 cm.

278. Vase, terracotta, Gordion, 9th century BC. Height 10.1 cm.

279. Ram's head bucket (situla), bronze, the Great Tumulus at Gordion,
end of the 8th century BC. Height 22 cm.

280. Lion's head bucket (situla), bronze, the Great Tumulus at Gordion,
end of the 8th century BC. Height 22.3 cm.

283. Omphalos bowl (phiale) with petal decoration on body, bronze, Tumulus W at Gordion, end of the 8th century BC. Height 7.3 cm.

281. Omphalos bowl (phiale), bronze, the Great Tumulus at Gordion,
end of the 8th century BC. Height 15.7 cm.

282. Omphalos bowl (phiale), bronze, the Great Tumulus at Gordion,
end of the 8th century BC. Height 22.2 cm.

284. Omphalos bowl (phiale), bronze, the Great Tumulus at Gordion,
end of the 8th century BC. Height 5 cm.

285. Omphalos bowl (phiale) with petal decoration on body, bronze, Tumulus P at Gordion, end of the 8th century BC. Height 5.5 cm.

286. Vessel with tall handle, bronze, the Great Tumulus at Gordion, end of the 8th century BC. Height 5.6 cm.

287. Vessel with bobbin-shaped handle, bronze, the Great Tumulus at Gordion, end of the 8th century BC. Height 8.8 cm.

288. Cauldron decorated with four handles in the shape of sirens, bronze, the Great Tumulus at Gordion, end of the 8th century BC. Height 51.5 cm.

289. Handle detail, viewed from the back.

290. Handle detail, viewed from the front.

291. Jug with trefoil mouth, bronze, the Great Tumulus at Gordion, end of the 8th century BC. Height 16.5 cm.

293. Small cauldron, bronze, the Great Tumulus at Gordion, end of the 8th century BC. Height 16 cm.

292. Jug with trefoil mouth, bronze, the Great Tumulus at Gordion, end of the 8th century BC. Height 35 cm.

295. One-handled mug, bronze, Tumulus W at
Gordion,
end of the 8th century BC. Height 16 cm.

294. Spouted jug, bronze, the Great Tumulus at
Gordion,
end of the 8th century BC. Height 14 cm.

296. One-handled vessel, bronze, the Great Tumulus at
Gordion,
end of the 8th century BC. Height 18 cm.

297. Inscribed bowl, bronze, the Great Tumulus at Gordion, end of the 8th century BC. Height 8 cm.

298. Detail of the inscription below the rim.

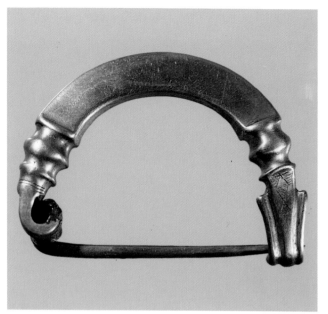

300. Fibula, electrum, Gordion, 8th century BC. Height 3.4 cm.

299. Dress-pins (fibulae), bronze, the Great Tumulus at Gordion, end of the 8th century BC. Height 5.0 - 6.5 cm.

301. Model of a four-horse chariot (quadriga), bronze, Tumulus P at Gordion, end of the 8th-beginning of the 7th century BC. Length 16 cm. Probably a toy, since the tomb belongs to a child from the royal family.

302. Statuette of Midas, terracotta, Gordion. Height 9.5 cm.

303. Statue of Cybele, limestone, Boğazköy, mid-6th century BC. Height 126 cm. Found in the forecourt before one of the gateways of the Phrygian-period Great Castle. The goddess is flanked by small figures of musicians playing a flute and a lyre. She represents an Iron Age continuation of the Anatolian cult of the Mother Goddess, symbolising fertility and prosperity. Here she is depicted with archaic features and wearing a tall head-dress (polos) and a pleated dress, all of which indicate Greek influence.

304 - 305. Painted reliefs depicting goats climbing up the Tree of Life and two warriors, terracotta, Pazarlı, 6th century BC. Height 31 and 44 cm.

306. Reconstruction of the decorative elements on the Phrygian building at Pazarlı.

307. Griffin relief, andesite, Ankara, 7th century BC. Height 98 cm.

308. Bull relief, andesite, Ankara, beginning of the 7th century BC. Height 104 cm.

309. Horse relief, andesite, Ankara, beginning of the 7th century BC. Height 110 cm.

310. Lion relief, andesite, Ankara, beginning of the 7th century BC. Height 110 cm.

311. Part of the frescoes that once decorated the long side walls of the assembly hall (apadana) at Altıntepe near Erzincan, end of the 8th-beginning of the 7th century BC. Two winged mythical figures stand flanking a stylised Tree of Life.

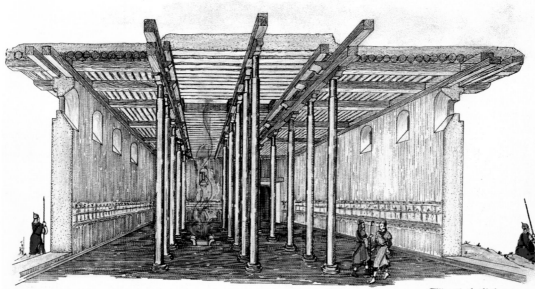

312. Artist's impression of the Altıntepe assembly hall.

URARTIANS

The Urartians established a state in the region of Lake Van in the early 1st millennium B.C. At its most powerful the state of Urartu had a large territory in the land between lake Urmia and the Euphrates valley, extending from Gökçegöl in south Transcaucasia to the Araxes valley and from the east coast of the Black Sea to the borders of Assyria. The land of Urartu comprised plains and plateaus surrounded by high and rocky mountains with deep, narrow valleys. The Urartians, who had to adjust to harsh natural conditions, were successful in agriculture and animal husbandry. Eastern Anatolia, which supported agriculture and stock breeding as well as having rich sources of minerals, had attracted the attention of Mesopotamian peoples since very ancient times. Because of its wealth it was attacked many times by the Assyrians. The Urartians, who had to resist these attacks, became unified at the beginning of the 1st millennium B.C. and established the state of Urartu. The centre of this state was at modern Van (Tuşpa).

The name "Urartians" who disappeared after invasions from the north by Medes and Scythians in the 6th century B.C., first occurs in the 8th century B.C. in the records of Shalmaneser I, a king of Assyria. These were written in cuneiform script. The people of Urartu were neither Semitic nor Indo - European. Studies carried out on the Urartian language show that it was a dialect of the Hurrian language. A Hurrian civilization that was contemporary with the Hittites existed in east and south - east Anatolia, stretching westwards as far as Antalya. It covered some of the same territory as the Kingdom of Urartu 500 years before the foundation of the Urartian states. Thus it should be accepted that the Urartians were descendants of the Hurrian race. At first, Urartu was influenced by Assyria and used the Assyrian script and language. It became possible to read the Urartian cuneiform script because of two bilingual inscriptions on which the same texts were given in both Assyrian and Urartian. There are also a few official or commercial letters written in Urartian on clay tablets. The written records of Urartu, however, were rather stilted, compared to those of Assyria. Urartian tablets written in cuneiform script mainly comprise legal contracts and letter. They are very few in number. The most important inscriptions are on stone, carved either on rock faces or on masonry blocks. They also had a script composed of figures like Hittite hieroglyphs. Urartian cuneiform records tell of the victories of Urartian kings, the slaves and spoils captured, and the building of canals, castles and sanctuaries. All these were specialties of the Urartians whose great accomplishments included the construction of water channels, making artificial lake, irrigation works and the draining of swamps. This is confirmed in the

Assyrian records. In their reports the kings of Assyria mentioned the fertility of Urartu and the wealth of the temples and royal treasuries.

The theocratic Urartian state was governed by a feudal system. In areas near the borders there were small city states governed by individual rulers, as in the earlier Hittite Empire. These rulers, who paid tax to the kingdom, were autonomous within their lands. They lived in fortified castles and in times of war their armies were put under the command of the Urartian kings.

Urartu reached the height of its power in the 9th or 8th centuries B.C. Although their kingdom was very mountainous, the Urartians tried to regulate the environment by public works, constructing dams and water channels. Besides these public works, the fine palaces and temples demonstrate the advanced level of architecture they possessed.

They cleverly adapted their monumental buildings to their surroundings. These were usually erected on very steep hillsides and carefully constructed of stones weighing 20 to 25 tons. Urartian architecture developed differently from that of Assyria. Urartian structures usually had stone foundations and long wooden beams. The temples, palaces, administrative build-ing and castles with their workshops and storerooms were surrounded by city walls with many towers. These structures are examples of their monumental architecture which combines setting, plan and construction techniques. The structures unearthed by the excavation of Altıntepe, Çavuştepe, Adilcevaz and Kayalıdere and elsewhere are important examples of the construction works mentioned in the inscriptions of Urartian Kings. The temples and the palaces, with their multi - columned reception halls, mark the contribution of Urartu to the history of architecture. Altıntepe is the best example of this type. Another important feature of Urartian art is the wall - painting. Although the wall - paintings which adorn Urartian official buildings and monumental structures show strong influences from Assyrian art, they display differences in both pattern and style. The wall - paintings combine geometric and plant motifs with various animal scenes, all worked out in bright colours. From these wall - paintings, which date to the second half of the 8th century B.C. and the first half of the 7th century B.C., we gain an insight into the artistic interests of the Urartians. Although they lived in the harsh environment of eastern Anatolia, the most popular scenes on these wall paintings comprise plant and geometric motifs, sacred trees flanked by winged griffons, winged sphinxes, gods on sacred animals, animal contest scenes and various animal motifs. The use of bright colours make the paintings vivid. Red, blue, beige, black, white, and, very rarely, green were used in these paintings.

The helmets and shields that have survived bear the names of the kings who owned them. They are decorated with various figural and animal motifs. A bronze cauldron from Altıntepe had four bulls' head attachments. This cauldron belongs to the early 7th century B.C. Bronze cauldrons adorned with figures in typical Urartian style were exported to Phrygia, Greece and Italy. Decorated bronze panels, also had an important place in Urartian art. Belts, helmets, shields, votive plaques, harnesses and quivers can be included in this group. The most important characteristic features of the belts lie in the symmetry and repetition of the motives.

Seals constitute another important aspect of Urartian art. As well as stamp seals and cylinder seals, there are cylindrically shaped stamp seals. These show us that Urartian innovations were made with regard to seals. The seals portray animal, plant and composite animal motifs.

A tradition of ivory carving was also carefully preserved. Most of the ivory pieces found are fragments from furniture, and they demonstrate the importance of ivory. Among the finds of ivory are bird - headed winged griffons, human faces, stags in relief, plaques decorated with palmets, carved clasped hands and lion figurines. Among these the statuette of a crouching lion from a tripod stool in the largest lion figurine from the Near East.

Assyrian influences on the tomb chamber of the Urartian kings were considerable. The subterranean burial chambers of the Urartian rulers were hewn out of the rock. The bodies of the dead were placed in wooden or stone sarcophagi. Next to the burial chambers but very near the surface were simple rock - cut tombs and urn emplacement. It is thought that the kings' servants and slaves were buried in such places. There were, however, some urn emplacements in the burial chambers, which show us that both inhumation and cremation were practiced at the funerals of royalty and common people alike.

There is a rich collection of Urartian finds from Altıntepe, Ağrı - Patnos, Van - Toprakkale, Muş - Kayalıdere and Adilcevaz in our Museum.

313. Inscribed vessel.

314. Short-necked vessel, bronze, Altıntepe, end of the 8th - beginning of the 7th century BC. Height 38.8 cm.

315. Cauldron on tripod stand, bronze, Altıntepe, end of the 8th - beginning of the 7th century BC. Height 51 cm.

316. Table, wood, Adicevaz,
8th century BC.
Height 43 cm.

317. Jug, bronze with leather
cover, purchased in eastern
Anatolia, 7th century BC.
Height 20 cm.

318. Bath-shaped coffin, bronze with leather cladding, purchased in eastern Anatolia, 7th century BC.
Height 56 cm.

319. Stemmed vessel, terracotta, Patnos, 8th century BC.
Height 22.1 cm.

321. Votive plaque, bronze, purchased in eastern Anatolia, 7th century BC. Height 15.7 cm.

320. Votive plaque, bronze, purchased in eastern Anatolia, 7th century BC. Height 11.4 cm.

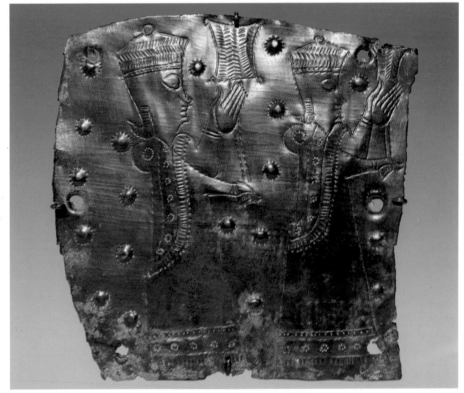

322. Votive plaque, bronze, purchased in eastern Anatolia, 7th century BC. Height 15.7 cm.

324. Lion statuette, bronze, Kayalıdere, end of the 8th - beginning of the 7th century BC. Height 6.4 cm.

325. Furniture legs, bronze, Kayalıdere, end of the 8th - beginning of the 7th century BC. Height 26 cm.

323. Quiver, bronze, Kayalıdere, end of the 8th - beginning of the 7th century BC. Length 62 cm.

197

326. Seated lion statuette, ivory with gold, Altıntepe, second half of the 8th century BC. Height 10 cm.

327. Winged mythical creature, ivory, Altıntepe, second half of the 8th century BC. Height 12.4 cm.

328. Lion statuette, ivory, Altıntepe, second half of the 8th century BC. Length 29.5 cm.

329. Mask, ivory, Altıntepe,
second half of the 8th
century BC.
Height 2.6 cm.

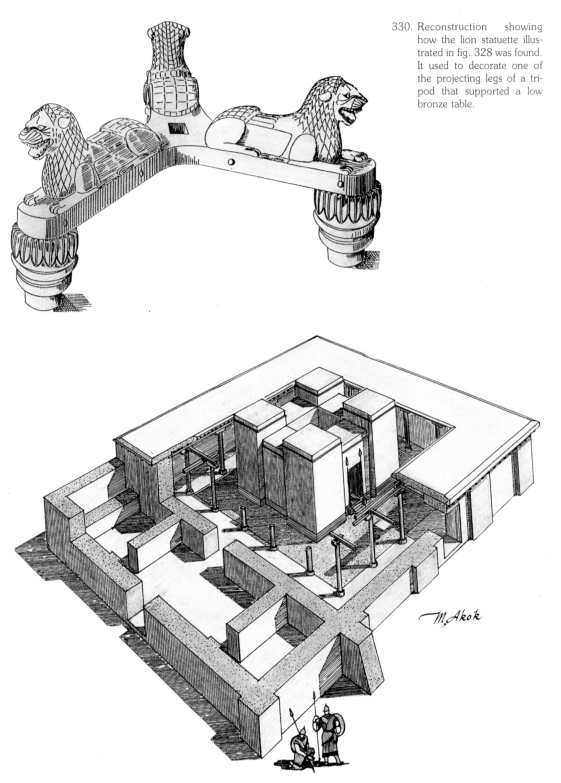

330. Reconstruction showing how the lion statuette illustrated in fig. 328 was found. It used to decorate one of the projecting legs of a tripod that supported a low bronze table.

M. Akok

331. Artist's impression of the Temple at Altıntepe.

332. Stamp seal, gold, Patnos, 8th century BC. Height 1.2 cm.

333. Cylinder seal, steatite, Patnos, 8th century BC. Height 3 cm.

334. Bell-shaped seal, bronze, Patnos, 8th century BC. Height 2.2 cm.

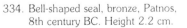

335. Relief plaque, gold,
Altıntepe, 8th century BC.
Height 2.6 cm.

336. Buttons, gold Altıntepe, end
of the 8th - beginning of the
7th century BC.
Height 0.5 cm.

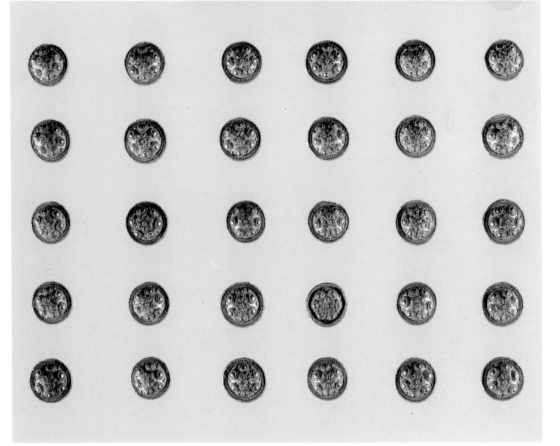

337. String of agate, amber and
blue stone beads, Patnos,
7th - 6th century BC.
Length 28.5 cm.

338. Earring, gold, Patnos,
7th - 6th century BC.
Height 5.6 cm.

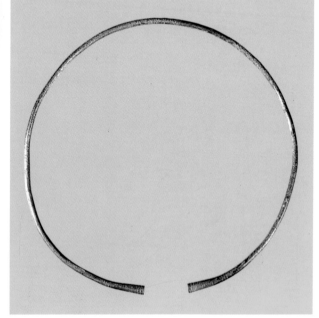

a   339. Necklace, silver, Patnos,
7th-6th century BC.
Diameter 13 cm.

341. Pin, silver, Patnos,
    7th - 6th century BC.
    Length 5.5 cm.

342. Bracelet, silver, Patnos,
    7t h - 6th century BC.
    Diameter 7.8 cm.

340. Pin, bronze, Patnos,
    7th century BC.
    Length 8.3 cm.

343. Vase with human face in relief, terracotta, Patnos, 9th-8th century BC. Height 14.6 cm.

344. Base decorated with reliefs and a cuneiform inscription, basalt, Kef Kalesi near Adilcevaz, 7th century BC. The main scene contains a pair of confronted figures of the winged god Haldi, each standing on a lion's back.

345. Incense burner, silver, İkiztepe near Uşak, 6th century BC. Height 28.8 cm.

LYDIAN PERIOD

The story of Lydian art has its roots in the Bronze Age, when the ancestors of the Lydian were in intermittently friendly and hostile contact with the Hittite Empire. Lydia continued with a splendid development in the Iron Age, especially under the Marmnad dynasty from Gypes to Croesus (685 - 547 BC.) Their Land Lydia become the most powerful kingdom after the death of phrygian king Midas in the Kimmerian raid on Gordion in ca. 695 BC. The Lydians preserved their own language and culture, but were open to contact with the west "Greeks" as well as East (Phrygians and luwians also Medas and Persians) and made diplomatic overtures as for as Egypt and Asyria.

Lydian art was heir to the best in the Anatolian tradition, and it become a source of inspiration and instruction for the art of their greatest Near Eastern rivals, the Achacmenid persians.

The strength of Lydian art is to have preserved authentic Anatolian heritage without prejudice and to have contributed its artists and craftsmen to the benefit of art and architecture as far as susa and pasargadess in persia and to have sent its precious jewellery and metal work to the sanctuones and courts of Greece, Lydia's contribution to ivory carving and the making of votive figurines will gradually become clearer with further discoveries.

The arts of sculpture and wall painting in the exhibition in the sphinxes supporting the line from the tomb chamber of the Kırkağaç - Horta Tumulus and in mutilated fragments of painting from Uşak - Aktepe Tumulus.

During the 1960's cultural artifacts from illegal excavations in western Anatolia were taken out of the country, these artifact has since been named the treasure of Karun or lydian Treasure.

The so-called "Lydian Treasure" includes objects made of precious metals such as gold and silver and consists of vessels, jewellery, figures, seals, wall-painting fragments and marble sphinxes. Most of these objects are now exhibited in the U.ak Museum. The metal objects in particular display a striking sophistication and consummate workmanship, using a variety of different techniques. The objects can be dated to the second half of the 6th century BC.

346. Oil bottle (aryballos) in the shape of a horse's head, İkiztepe near Uşak, 6th century BC. Height 7.65 cm.

347. Oil bottle (aryballos) in the shape of a warrior's head, İkiztepe near Uşak, 6th century BC. Height 6.1 cm.

348. Lidded box (pyxis), white marble, İkiztepe near Uşak, 6th century BC. Diameter 8.9 cm.

349. Perfume bottle (alabastron), alabaster, İkiztepe near Uşak, 6th century BC. Height 20.8 cm.

350. Spouted jug, silver, İkiztepe near Uşak,
6th century BC. Height 11.6 cm.

351. Bowl (phiale), silver, İkiztepe near Uşak,
6th century BC. Height 3.7 cm.

352. One-handled strainer bowl, silver, İkiztepe
near Uşak, 6th century BC. Height 3 cm.

353. Two-handled jar (amphora), terracotta, Kültepe, Hellenistic period. Height 31 cm. The vessel is covered with a white slip and then richly painted in black and red. On the neck is a pattern of fish scales, while the shoulder is decorated with a wavy pattern of ivy tendrils. On the body is depicted a beardless hunts-man mounted on a rearing horse. His tunic is rendered with naturalistic folds.

THE ANATOLIAN CIVILIZATIONS FROM 1200 B. C. TO PRESENT

There were major changes in Anatolia in the wake of the Aegean migrations, which took place at the end of the second millennium. This event brought - about the fall of the Hittite Empire and in the first half of the 1st millennium B. C., late Hittites, Urartians and Phrygians, who had established kingdoms in different areas of Anatolia, took over control. At the same period, the Greek people arrived in Western Anatolia, via islands, as a result of the disruptions caused by the Dorian Migrations. After settling in Western Anatolia, they unified with local people and established the foundations of the Ionian civilizations. In this way the first colony settlements were founded. This period is characterized by motifs drawn by compasses and is called the "PROTOGEOMETRIC AGE" (1100 - 950 B. C.). Then it is followed by the "GEOMETRIC AGE", represented with the alteration of round shaped motifs into angular ones.

The art, which has been always important in Ionia, had witnessed major developments, both in terms of architectural and sculptural characteristics, under the oriental influences. The foundations of giant temples were established in this period. The anatomical characteristics of the human body were worked out more realistically on the sculptural work in comparison with the ones from protogeometric or geometric ages. Big marble statues were first made in 670 B. C. and the painted pottery of the Eastern Greeks, which were decorated with animal friezes, continued to be produced under the vigorous influences of Anatolia.

The big - sized pieces of art produced during the Archaic period, a continuation of the orientalising style, also establishes the characteristics of this style to a certain extent. The statues and the Ionian architecture of the Western Anatolian culture of this period established the infrastructure of the "Classical Age" of the Western Aegean.

There were Carian and Lycian civilizations in the southwestern Anatolia during 700 - 300 B. C. The rock tombs of these civilizations are the most distinguished traces which were left by them in this region of Anatolia. On the other hand, the control of central Anatolia was under the Lydian Kingdom and the centre of the Kingdom was at Sardis. By extending their boundary upto Kızılırmak, they took over the control of Phrygians and owing to good relations with Ionian city states, they also included Ephesus into their territory and became the most powerful state of the region. They minted the first metal coin in the seventh century B. C., and re-proved their importance.

After Lydia was vanquished by the Persian Empire in 546 B. C., the civilizations in western Anatolia intermingled with Greek and Persian civilizations resulting in the creation of a Greco - Persian style.

This situation was ended with the invasion of Anatolia by Alexander the Great, and a new period called "HELLENISTIC" started (330 - 30 B. C.). After the death of Alexander the Great, as result of the internal struggles between his generals this powerful kingdom was shared by them, and most of Anatolia entered the rule of the Pergamon Kingdom. Later according to the will of the last Pergamon King, western Anatolia entered the rule of Romans.

Anatolia, which became a part of the Roman Empire by means of a will, was Romanized by peace rather than war, and continued to preserve its own traditional cultural characteristics. These regional characteristics were dominant even in the most powerful periods of the Roman Empire.

When the Roman Empire split into two, the old Greek city "Byzantion" became the capital of the Eastern Roman Empire (330 B. C.) and received the name of "Constantinopolis" in honour of the name of the Emperor. Byzantine art is a mixture of Roman art, which came into being in Anatolia with dominant regional characteristics, with the characteristics of Christianity. The Byzantium civilization had a life of nearly thousand years in the span of time between the 4th and 15th centuries.

The Oğuz Turks, who had been living at the west of Transoxiana, accepted the Moslem religion in the 10th century and in order to spread it, they started raids to Byzantine territory. The Malazgirt Battle, which took place in 1071, opened the doors of Anatolia to Turks. The Seljuk Turks, who arrived in İznik and accepted it as their capital, turned Anatolia to a province of the Great Seljuk State. After the collapse of the Great Seljuk State, the Anatolian Seljuk State was established and the capital was moved to Konya.

The Anatolian Seljuk State came to an end as a result of the Mongol invasions and Anatolia entered the rule of İlkhanid Turks. For a span of time it was governed by different Turkish rulers, then living in different regions of Anatolia (1071 - 1300).

On the arrival of the Kayı Tribe of Oğuz Turks in Anatolia, the Seljuks Sultan showed the Söğüt area near Byzantine territory as a place for them to settle down. Thus the foundations of an Empire, which would continue for 600 years was established. Expanding their borders, the descendants of Osman captured Bursa and made it the capital. After sometime they captured the Byzantine lands on Thrace and moved their capital to Edirne. In 1453 İstanbul became the capital and turned out to be a culture and art city. Ottoman art is a synthesis of the Turkish - Islamic art and Anatolian culture. The building, which you are now in, is one of the beautiful examples of Ottoman architecture (1299 - 1923).

Towards the end of the 19th century, the Ottoman Empire became very weak and thus occupied from four sides. In 1919 the Independence War started and in 1923 the Turkish Republic was declared.

354. Hand mirror, gilded bronze, purchased, from Tokat, 1st century BC-1st century AD. Diameter 10.6 cm.

355. Diadem, gold, 3rd century BC. Length 30.3 cm.

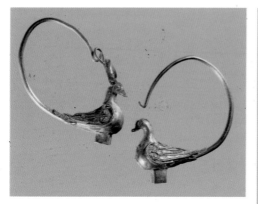

356. Pair of earrings, each decorated with the figure
of a dove, gold, 4th-3rd century BC.
Height 3.2 cm.

357. Earring decorated with the figure of a sphinx, gold,
4th century BC. Height 2.1 cm.

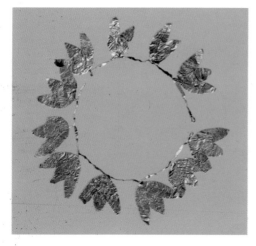

358. Diadem, gold, 1st century BC. Length 27 cm.

359. Necklace, gold, 1st century BC-1st century AD. Length 41.5 cm.

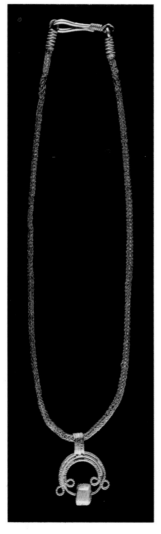

360. Earring, gold and coloured glass, 4th-3rd century BC. Height 4.5 cm.

361. Earring, gold, end of the 4th century BC. Length 3.6 cm.

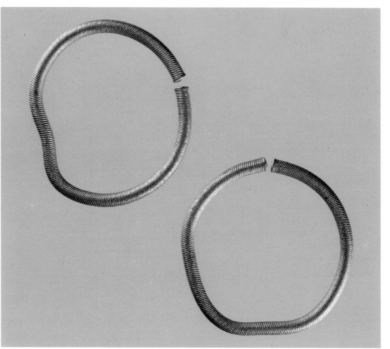

362. Pair of bracelets, gold, Yozgat, 4th century BC. Diameter 7.2 cm.

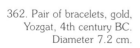

363. Perfume bottle (alabastron), glass, purchased,
5th century BC. Height 12.2 cm.

365. Perfume bottle (alabastron), glass, purchased,
first half of the 5th century BC.
Height 10.6 cm.

364. Small two-handled jar (amphoriskos), glass, Taşköprü,
end of the 2nd century BC. Height 15 cm.

366. Ribbed bowl (phiale), glass, 1st century AD. Height 5.6 cm.

368. Medallion (phalera), glass, purchased, first half of the 1st century AD. Diameter 3.8 cm.

367. Drinking cup (rhyton), glass, 1st century AD. Height 12.3 cm.

369. A selection of glass vessels of various shapes.

219

370. Portrait head, bronze, Kahramanmaraş, first half of the 2nd century AD. Height 37 cm.

371. Statuette of Herakles, bronze, purchased, from Yozgat, Roman period. Height 11.5 cm.

372. Statuette of Zeus, bronze, purchased, from Zonguldak, Roman period. Height 10.2 cm.

373. Bull figurine, bronze, purchased, Roman period.
Height 9.5 cm.

374. Eagle figurine, bronze,
İliara near Karaman,
Roman period.
Height 6.8 cm.

375. Stag figurine, bronze, purchased,
from Safranbolu,
Roman period.
Height 6.4 cm.

376. Electrum nomisma, minted at Kyzikos in Mysia, 500-450 BC. Diameter 2.1 cm.

377. Silver stater, minted at Chalcedon in Bithynia, mid-4th century BC. Diameter 2.2 cm.

378. Gold octodrachm, minted by Seleukos III, King of Syria, 226-223 BC. Diameter 3 cm.

379. Silver denarius, minted by Q. Voconius Vitulus at Rome, 40 BC. Diameter 1.9 cm.

380. Bronze sestertius of the emperor Domitian, minted at Rome, AD 81-96. Diameter 3.6 cm.

381. Silver cistophoric tetradrachm of the emperor Claudius, AD 41-54. Diameter 2.7 cm.

382. Bronze follis of the emperor
Justinian, AD 527-565. Diameter
4.15 cm.

383. Silver histamenon of the emperor
Romanus III, AD 1028-1034.
Diameter 2.7 cm.

384. Gold scyphate of the emperor of
Michael VII, AD 1071-1078.

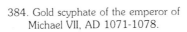

385. Silver dinar of the Seljuk sultan
Giyas-ed-din Keyhüsrev,
AD 1236-1246.
Diameter 2.3 cm.

386. Gold coin of the Ottoman sultan
Mehmet II the Conqueror,
AD 1451-1481.
Diameter 2 cm.

387. Gold coin commemorating the
100th anniversary of Atatürk's birth,
minted in 1981.
Diameter 3 cm.

388. Statuette of Aphrodite and Eros, terracotta, Roman period. Height 30 cm.

389. Statuette of Aphrodite, terracotta, Kütahya (Cotiaeum), Roman period. Height 26 cm.

390. Lamp, terracotta, purchased,
Roman period.

392. Lamp, bronze, purchased,
Byzantine period. Height 37.5 cm.

391. Lamp, terracotta, purchased,
Roman period.

393. Votive stele, marble, Emirdağ near Afyon,
2nd - 3rd century AD. Height 27 cm.

394. Votive stele, marble, Altıntaş near
Kütahya, 2nd - 3rd century AD.
Height 28.9 cm.

395. Votive steles, marble. Height 19.9, 22.9 and 14. 8 cm.

396. Votive steles, marble, Emirdağ near Afyon,
2nd - 3rd century AD. Height 28.9, 18.3 and 27.4 cm.

398. Winged Eros, marble, Roman period.

397. Head from a statue, marble, Roman period.

399. Statue of Hygeia, marble, Roman period.

400. Oil flasks (lekythoi),
terracotta, Konya
area,
5th - 4th century BC.
Height 13.1 and 7.7
cm.

401. Bowl (lebes), wine jug
(oinochoe) and oil
flask (lekythos), terra-
cotta, Salihli near
Sinop,
5th - 4th century BC.
Height 17, 16.2 and 7.7
cm.

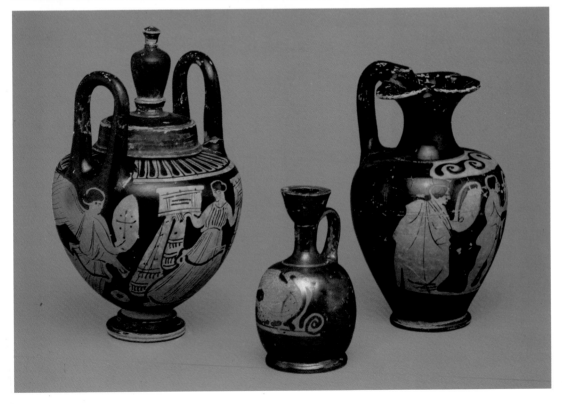

402. Two-handled red figure
     vase (pelike), terracotta,
     Sinop excavations,
     5th - 4th century BC.
     Height 30 cm.

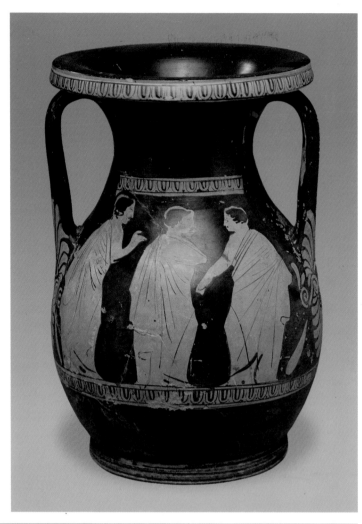

403. Drinking cup (kan-
     tharos), terracotta,
     Salihli near Sinop,
     Hellenistic period.
     Height 9.6 cm.

404. Mortar, bronze, 13th century AD.

405. Jug, terracotta, 13th century AD.
Height 20 cm.

406. Glazed wall tile,
Seljuk palace at
Kubad-abad near
Beyşehir, Konya,
17th century AD.
Height 27.1 cm.

407. Glazed wall tile, 17th century AD.
Height 19.8 cm.

408. Glazed wall tile, 17th century AD. Height 20 cm.

409. Examples of modern Iznik-style pottery made at Kütahya.

410. Sculpture known as "The Boar Hunt", found in Ankara, fine-grained marble, 2nd century AD.
Height 83 cm.

ANKARA THROUGH THE AGES

Ankara, the capital of the Turkish Republic, is located in Anatolia at the cross roads of main highways connecting east to west and north to south.

The Prehistoric settlements discovered in Ankara and its vicinity indicate that the area was continually settled since ancient times. Various artifacts belonging to the Palaeolithic era were discovered in the settlement of Etiyokuşu, near Çubukçayı, as well as in Ergazi on the İstanbul - Ankara highway and in the Maltepe districts. The remains of small palaces belonging to the Chalcolithic era and Bronze Age unearthed in Ahlatlıbel to the southwest of Ankara and in Koçumbeli indicate the existence of principalities in the Prehistoric ages. It is known that later Ankara and its vicinity were captured by the Hittites who settled in the city. A Hittite settlement was discovered in Bitik near the Mürted Plain. In Gavurkale near the town of Haymana, 60 km. southwest of Ankara, there is an area sacred to the Hittites. Another important Hittite settlement again in Haymana near the Oyaca Village is Külhöyük. This settlement is being excavated by the Anatolian Civilizations Museum.

The first important settlement in Ankara was thus during the Phrygian times. Excavations showed that this Phrygian town in Ankara occupied the land between the Temple of Augustus and the Roman Bath and its vicinity. According to legend, the town was founded by the Phrygian king Midas. Phrygians named the town Ankyra which means "Anchor". Remains from excavated tumuli in Ankara and its vicinity indicate the existence of Phrygian settlement in Ankara between 750 - 500 BC.

The capital city of the Phrygians was Gordion, in the area of Polatlı, near Yassıhöyük village, 96 km. southwest of Ankara. There are more than one hundred tumuli in Gordion area. The city mound and twenty five tumuli, among which was the Great Tumulus, have been excavated. Numerous works of art from here give as important information on Phrygian art and culture, between the 8th and 5th centuries BC.

There is not much information on the period between the Phrygian age and the age of the Macedonian king Alexander the Great. It is known only that the city located on the famous King's Road built in the time of Dareios I (522 - 486 BC.), the king of Persia, was an important trade center. Alexander the Great spent the winter of 334 - 333 BC. In Gordion and came to Ankyra in the spring and waited the Persian army until autumn.

The Tektosages, a tribe of the Galatians who, in 278 - 277 BC., came to Anatolia from Europe in three tribes and settled in the area within the arch of the Halys (Kızılırmak) river near Ankara and Pessinus, made Ankara their capital. Roman general G. Manlius Vulso came to Ankyra in 189 BC. and defeated the Galatians in a battle near the town. On the condition that the Galatians stop looting and stay within the borders of their land, Vulso agreed to leave them under the rule of the Kingdom of Pergamon.

In 133 BC. when the Kingdom of Pergamon was bequeathed to the Romans, the Galatians, who remained within the lands of Great Phrygia, were given to the Pontic Kingdom. Yet, the Pontic Kingdom never succeeded in becoming a powerful nation especially in the lands near Ankara.

Following a period of confusion, the Roman emperor Augustus in 25 BC. included Galatia under Roman rule and therefore Ankyra became the capital of Galatia, a Roman province. The city was renamed Sebaste (honourable) in honour of Augustus, who later built a temple here. Due to its strategic location at the Junction of the roads connecting the eastern border of the Roman Empire to Europe, Ankyra under Roman role developed fast and became a major military base where the emperors and armies rested. Especially in the 2nd century AD, the town lived through a golden age. In the early 3rd century AD. Emperor

Caracalla repaired the walls of the castle and built a bath complex at the foot of the castle.

In the middle of the 4th century AD., as Christianity spread, Ankyra gained prominence and became a religious center. In 314 and 458 AD. The Ecumenical Council met here and many important religious decisions were made during these meetings. In 362 AD. Emperor Julian spent some time in Ankyra and set new regulations to improve the administration of the city. When the ROman Empire split in 395 AD. The city was acquired by the Eastern Roman Empire.

Under the Byzantine rule, Ankyra lived through a period of peace until the 7th century AD. When Arab invasions began. The Seljuk Sultan Alpaslan defeated the Byzantine army in Malazgirt in 1071, and in 1073 Ankara came under Turkish rule. The reign of Sultan Alaaddin Keykubat was the golden age (1219 - 1237) of the Suljuks. During this time Ankara was reconstructed extensively.

During the Mongol invasion, like the other Seljuks cities, Ankara was destroyed too, and the Seljuk Sultan Gıyasettin Keyhüsrev II, who was defeated, came to Ankara to take refuge in the well - fortified castle. Beginning in 1243, Anatolian Seljuk State started losing land to the

Mongols and the Seljuks rulers lost their power. Finally, in 1304 Ankara, too, came under the rule of the Mongols and from then on it was administered by state governors called Ahi Beys who, under the supervision of Mongols, carried on trade.

During the Islamic are, the name of Ankyra was changed to Engürü and Angora. The city was captured by the Ottomans in 1356 and the Ottoman Sultan Murad I ruled from Ankara in 1362 - 1363. Tamerlane, in 1402, invaded Anatolia and Yıldırım Beyazıd was defeated by Tamerlane in the Battle of Ankara which took place in the Çubuk Plain. During the expansion of the Ottoman Empire, upon the establishment of state rule, Ankara became a centre of the Anatolian states.

In the beginning of the 17th century Ankara witnessed revolts by the Celalis who lived in the area. Many sections of the city were destroyed during these riots. As in the other towns in Anatolia, during the decline of the Ottoman Empire very little happened in Ankara. During this period it succeeded in maintaining its importance in the area as a center for trade. Especially mohair, and different kinds of fabric were the main items for trade. Tannery was important too.

During the collapse of the Ottoman Empire and the War of Independence, the city started to gain importance. Following the victory at the end of the War of Independence, on October 13, 1923, Ankara became the capital of the Turkish Republic.

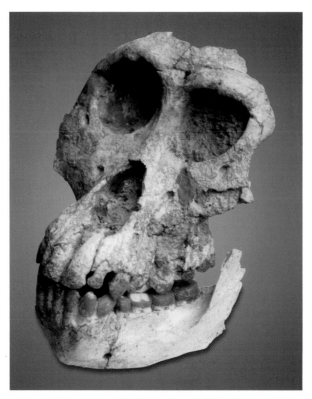

411. "Ankara Ape" (Ankarapithecus), Sinap Formation
Excavations near Kazan, Ankara, Miocene period.

412. View of the Sinap Formation Excavations near Kazan, Ankara.

415. Beak-spouted mug, terracotta, Karaoğlan, mid - 3rd millennium BC. Height 14.6 cm.

413. Idol and toys in the shape of animals, terracotta, Ankara area, mid - 3rd millennium BC.

414. Beak-spouted jug, bronze, Haymana near Ankara, mid - 3rd millennium BC. Height 12.8 cm.

416. Two-handled drinking cup (depas amphikypellon), terracotta, Karaoğlan, mid - 3rd millennium BC. Height 24.2 cm.

418. Seal (bulla), terracotta, Külhöyük,
18th - 17th century BC.
Height 1.4 cm.

417. View of the excavations at Külhöyük.

419. Stamp seal, stone, Külhöyük,
18th - 17th century BC.
Height 2.8 cm.

420. Impression of the stamp seal illustrated in fig. 419.

422. A selection of finds from Külhöyük, terracotta,
18th - 17th century BC.

421. Feeding bottle, terracotta, Külhöyük,
18th - 17th century BC. Height 21 cm.

423. Drinking horn (rhyton), terracotta, Bitik, 14th - 13th century BC. Length 25 cm.

424. Painted vessels, terracotta, Ankara area, 8th century BC. Height 14.4, 13.7 and 8.8 cm.

425. Painted jug with trefoil mouth, 8th century BC.
Height 20.9 cm.

426. Jug with trefoil mouth, terracotta, Gordion,
8th century BC.

427. Female head from a statue, marble, from the excavation of the Roman theatre in Ankara, 2nd century AD. Height 40 cm.

428. Satyr, marble, the Roman theatre in Ankara, 2nd century AD.

429. Diadem, gold, from the excavations at Balgat in Ankara, 1st-2nd century AD. Weight 62.04 gr.

431. Finger ring with stone bezel, gold, Balgat excavations, 1st-2nd century AD. Diameter 2.86 cm.

430. Flask, bronze, Balgat excavations, 1st-2nd century AD. Height 19.9 cm.

432. Glass vessels from the Balgat excavations, 1st - 2nd century AD.

435. Vessel decorated with the head of a crocodile, terracotta, Ulus, Ankara, Roman period. Height 4.2 cm.

433. Necklace, gold, Ulus, Ankara, late Roman period.

434. Heads from figurines, terracotta, Ulus, Ankara, Roman period.

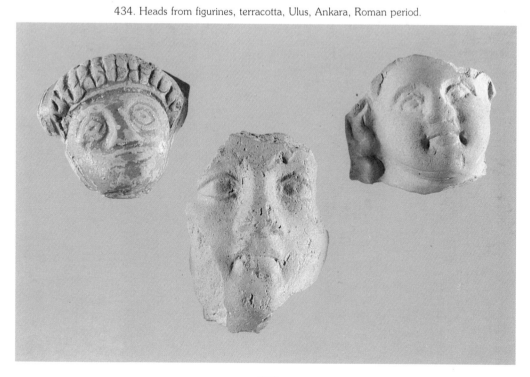

436. Vessels from the Ankara area, terracotta, Roman period.
Height 8.2 and 10.8 cm.

438. Large vessel, terracotta, Kazan near
Ankara, Roman period.
Height 42 cm.

437. Horseman figurines (toys), terracotta,
1st century BC-1st Century AD.

439. Mên, the Moon God, marble, found in Yenimahalle,
Ankara, Roman period. Height 64.5 cm.

440. Vespasian (AD 69-79), bronze.
Diameter 3.2 cm.

441. Trajan (AD 98-117), bronze.
Diameter 3.2 cm.

442. Lucius Verus (AD 161 - 169),
bronze.

443. Bust of the emperor Trajan as a tondo, Ankara, beginning of the 2nd century AD. Diameter 63 cm.

444. Statuette of the Mother Goddess Cybele, terracotta, Gordion, Hellenistic period. Height 14.5 cm.

445. Head of a rider, marble, Gordion, Hellenistic period. Height 13.7 cm.

446. Female head, marble, Ankara, 1st-2nd century AD. Height 13.1 cm.

447. Veiled female head, marble, Ankara, 2nd-3rd century AD. Height 32 cm.

449. Statuette of Asklepios, marble, Kütlüdüğün near Ankara, 2nd century AD. Height 28.5 cm.

448. Statuette of Athena, marble, Kütlüdüğün near Ankara, 2nd century AD. Height 34.5 cm.

450. Bust of Zeus, marble, Ankara, 1st-2nd century AD. Height 102 cm.

EDİRNE
KIRKLARELİ
ZONGULDAK
KASTAMONU
İSTANBUL
TEKİRDAĞ
KOCAELİ
11
BOLU
40
19
SAKARYA
İznik
ÇANKIRI
CORUM
Lapseki
İnandık 27
28 Kalın
ÇANAKKALE
BURSA
BİLECİK
18
Etiyokuşu
4 Alacahöyük
Troya
Daskilaion
Bozhöyük
25 Ilıca
22
10
Neandreia
ANKARA
Hasanoğlan
Boğazköy
Assos
Anıtkabir
7
3
Ahlatlıbel
KIRIKKALE
BALIKESİR
ESKİŞEHİR
20 Gordion
Karaoğlan
Bergama
KÜTAHYA
30
Kaman
Çandarlı
Myrina
Karayavşan 31
Kyme
İkiztepe 26
Yanarlar
Kulu
KIRŞEHİ
Bayraklı
MANİSA
Emirdağ 16
Şereflikochisar
Erythrai
UŞAK
AFYON
42 Sultan
İZMİR
Sardis
NEVŞEHİR
9 Beycesultan
Efes
Köylütolu 35
Acemhöyük
Priene
Magnesia
DENİZLİ
AKSARAY
Milet
Alabanda
BURDUR
ISPARTA
KONYA
13
NİĞ
Didyma
Aphrodisias
Çatalhöyük
Karapınar
Lagina
Beyşehir
MUĞLA
21 Hacılar
Çumra
Ereğli
Bodrum
KARAMAN
29 Karain
12 Canhasan
ANTALYA
Perge
Yümüktepe
Tar
15 Elmalı
İÇEL

OP

SAMSUN
MERZİFON 45
Ünye
AMASYA
Horoztepe 24
Mahmatlar 37
ışathöyük
TOKAT

ORDU
GİRESUN

TRABZON
RİZE

ARTVİN

GÜMÜŞHANE

KARS

BAYBURT
Karaz 32
ERZURUM

İğdır

SİVAS

ERZİNCAN
Altıntepe 6

AĞRI

ar 5
Havuzköy 23

Kültepe 36
KAYSERİ

TUNCELİ
BİNGÖL
Kayalıdere 33

39 Patnos
14
Çavuştepe

Adilcevaz
2

ELAZIĞ
MUŞ

VAN 46
44
Toprakkale

Aslantepe 8
Çayönü
MALATYA

BİTLİS
Tilkitepe 43

ADIYAMAN
DİYARBAKIR
BATMAN
SİİRT

KAHRAMANMARAŞ
Karatepe
Sakçagözü 41
GAZİANTEP
Osmaniye
Zincirli 34
Kargamış

ŞANLIURFA
MARDİN
ŞIRNAK
HAKKARİ

Dörtyol

ATAY
Tel Açana
ndağı

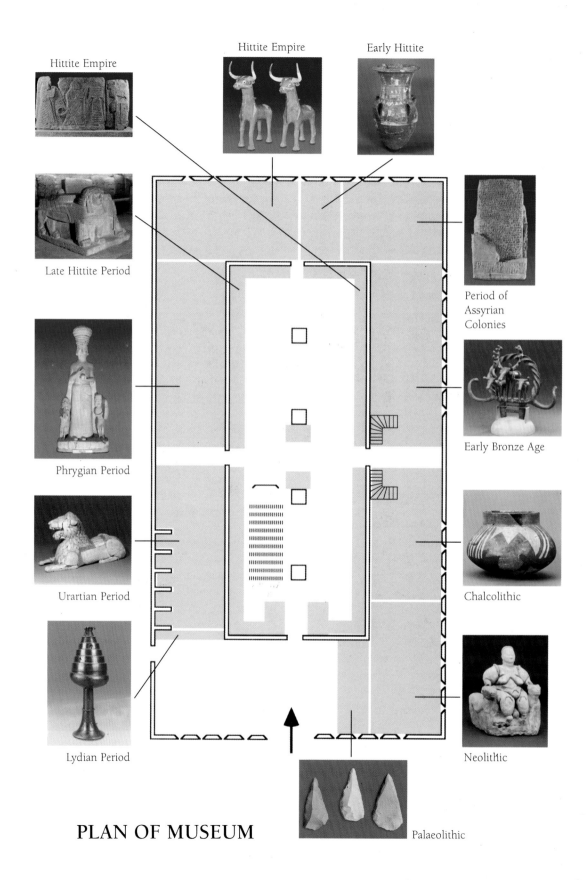

Hittite Empire

Hittite Empire

Early Hittite

Late Hittite Period

Period of Assyrian Colonies

Phrygian Period

Early Bronze Age

Urartian Period

Chalcolithic

Lydian Period

Neolithic

Palaeolithic

PLAN OF MUSEUM

Ankara

Classical Period

GROUND FLOOR PLAN OF MUSEUM

CHRONOLOGIE OF ANATOLIA

Prehistoric Periods

PALAEOLITHIC	
NEOLITHIC	8000 - 5500
CHALCOLITHIC	5500 - 3000
EARLY BRONZ AGE	3000 - 2000

Timeline scale (left): 400.000 · 8000 · 7000 · 6000 · 5000 · 4000 · 3000 · 2000 · 1000 · 0 · (B.C. / A.D.) · 1000 · 2000

Historic Periods

ASSYRIAN TRADE COLONIES	1950 - 1750
OLD HITTITE	1750 - 1450
HITTITE EMPIRE	1450 - 1200
NEW HITTITE	1200 - 700
PHRIGIAN "Early and Late Phase"	750 - 300
LYDIAN	700 - 300
URARTIAN	900 - 600
CARIAN / LYCIAN	700 - 300
İIONIAN	1050 - 300
PERSIAN	545 - 333
HELLENISTIC	333 - 30
ROMAN EMPIRE	B.C. 30 - 395
EARLY CHRISTIAN BYZANTIC PERIOD	330 - 1453
SELJUK PERIOD	1077 - 1308
OTTOMAN PERIOD	1299 - 1920
REPUBLIC	1920 -

FIND PLACES OF OBJECTS IN THE MUSEUM

FIND PLACE	No.	PALAEOLITHIC	NEOLITHIC	CHALCOLITHIC	EARLY BRONZ AGE	ASSYRIAN COLONIES	HITTITE	NEW HITTITE	PHRIGIAN	URARTIAN	LYDIAN
ACEMHÖYÜK	1					○	□				
ADİLCEVAZ	2									⬟	
AHLATLIBEL	3				●						
ALACAHÖYÜK	4			▲	●	○	□	△			
ALİŞAR	5			▲		○		△			
ALTINTEPE	6									⬟	
ANITKABİR	7							△			
ARSLANTEPE	8							◉			
BEYCESULTAN	9				●		□				
BOĞAZKÖY	10						□	△			
BOLU	11				●						
CANHASAN	12			▲							
ÇATALHÖYÜK	13		■								
ÇAVUŞTEPE	14									⬟	
ELMALI	15				●						
EMİRDAĞ	16				●						
ESKİYAPAR	17				●		□				
ETİYOKUŞU	18				●						
FERZANT	19				●		□				
GORDİON	20								△		
HACILAR	21		■	▲							
HASANOĞLAN	22				●						
HAVUZKÖY	23							◉			
HOROZTEPE	24				●						
ILICA	25						□				
İKİZTEPE	26										⊠
İNANDIK	27						□				
KALINKAYA	28				●						
KARAİN	29	✡									
KARAOĞLAN	30				●						
KARAYAVŞAN	31				●						
KARAZ	32			▲							
KAYALIDERE	33									⬟	
KARGAMIŞ	34							◉			
KÖYLÜTOLU	35						□				
KÜLTEPE	36				●	○	□				
MAHMATLAR	37				●						
MERZİFON	38				●						
PATNOS	39									⬟	
PAZARLI	40								△		
SAKÇAGÖZÜ	41							◉			
SULTANHAN	42							◉			
TİLKİTEPE	43									⬟	
TOPRAKKALE	44									⬟	
ÜNYE	45									⬟	
VAN	46									⬟	

BIBLIOGRAPHY

PREHISTORIC PERIODS
Paleolithic

BORDES, F. - **Le Paléolithique Dans le Monde.**
(1968) L'Univers des Connaissances, Paris, 1968

CHILDE, G. -**Man Makes Himself.**
(1956) Watts, London, 1956

CHILDE, G. -**Tarihte Neler oldu.**
(1974) (Çev. Alâeddin Şenel - Meten Tunçay) Odak Yayınları: 10, Tarih dizisi (T): 2 Ankara, 1974.

KANSU, Şevket Aziz: **"Stone Age Cultures in Turkey",**
American, Journal of Archaeology. vol. 51. 1947

KÖKTEN, I. Kılıç **"Antalya Karain Mağarasında Yapılan Tarih Öncesi Araştırmalarına Toplu Bir Bakış",** Türk Arkeoloji Dergisi VII-I

KÖKTEN, İ. K.- **"Karain'in Türkiye Prehistoryasındaki Yeri".**
T.C.D XVIII - XIX, Sayı 22-23, Ankara, 1964, s. 17-27

SEMENOV, Ś.A.- **Prehistoric Technology.**
(1964) (Translated by M.W Thompson) Cory, Adams - Mackay, London, 1964.

SOLECKI, R.S. **"The old world paleolithic"**
The Old World Early Man to the Development of Agriculture New York, 1974 pp. 45-70.

SOYLU, G.- **Prehistorik Devirlerde Avcılık ve Türkiye'deki İzleri.**
(1971) Yayınlanmamış Doktora tezi. Ankara, 1971

YALÇINKAYA, I.- **Taş Devirlerinde Sanat Eserleri ve Türkiye'deki İzleri** (1973) Yayınlanmamış Doktora tezi. Ankara, 1971

Neolithic Chalcolithic Early Bronze Age

ARIK. R.O.: **Türk Tarih Kurumu Tarafından Yapılan Alacahöyük Hafriyatı** 1935, Ankara. 1936

ARIK. R.O. **"Karaoğlan Hafriyatı"** Belleten III.. 1939

Avrupa Konseyi 18. Avrupa Sanat Sergisi, Anadolu Medeniyetleri, İstanbul. 1983, Tarih Öncesi / Hitit / İlk Demir Çağı, T.C. Kültür ve Turizm Bakanlığı.

BLEGEN. C.W. **"Troy I. General Introduction. The First and Second Settlements"** Princeton, 1950.
Troy II. The Third Fourth and Fifth Settlements, Princeton 1951

DOLUNAY, Necati: **"Hasanoğlan İdolü"** V. Türk Tarih Kongresi Raporu, TTK. Basımevi, Ankara 1960

FRENCH, D.H. **"Late Chalcolithic Pottery in North-West Turkey and The Aegean"**, Anatolian Studies, XI, 1961.

FRENCH, D.H.: **"Excavations at Can Hasan."** Anatolian Studies, XII, 1962; **"Excavations at Can Hasan : Second Preliminary Report, 1962"**, Anatolian Studies, XIII, 1963; **"Third Preliminary Report"**, Anatolian Studies, XIV. 1964; **"Fourth Preliminary Report, 1964"**, Anatolian Studies XV, 1965; **"Fifth Preliminary Report"**, Anatolian Studies. XVI, 1966

GÜTERBOCK, H.G.: **Halil Ethem Hatıra Kitabı, Ankara 1947**

KANSU. Şevket Aziz: **Etiyokuşu Hafriyatı Raporu** 1937, TTK, Basımevi, Ankara 1940.

KOŞAY, H. Z.: **Alacahöyük Kazısı 1936, Ankara, 1944**

KOŞAY, H.Z: **Türk Tarih Kurumu Tarafından Yapılan Alacahöyük Kazısı** 1937-1939'daki Çalışmalara ve Keşiflere Ait İlk Rapor, TTKY S.V. no. 5, Ankara 1951

KOŞAY H. Z.: **Akok, M., Türk Tarih Kurumu Tarafından Yapılan Alacahöyük Kazısı** 1940-1948'deki Çalışmalara ve Keşiflere Ait İlk Rapor, TTK Ys. V., no. 6, Ankara-1966

KOŞAY, H.Z.: **"Ahlatlıbel Hafriyatı"** Türk Tarih Arkeologya ve Etnoğrafya Dergisi, II, Ankara, 1934.

KOŞAY, H.Z ve TURFAN, K - **"Erzurum-Karaz Kazısı Raporu",** Belleten, XXIII, 1959.

KOŞAY, H.Z. ve VARY, H: **Pulur Kazısı Raporu,** Ankara, 1964

KOŞAY, H.Z. ve AKOK M.: **"Amasya Mahmatlar Köyü Definesi"** Belleten, XIV. 1950

LLOYD, S. ve MELLAART, J.: **Beycesultan I, The Chalcolithic and Early Bronze Age Levels,** London. 1962

MELLAART, James: **"Anatolian Chronology in the Early and Middle Bronze Age"**, Anatolian Studies, VII, 1957.

MELLAART, James: **"Early Cultures of the South Anatolian Plateau. The Late Chalcolithic and Early Bronze Ages in the Konya Plain"**, Anatolian Studies, XIII, 1963

MELLAART, James: **Çatalhöyük. A Neolithic Town in Anatolia,** London, 1967.

MELLAART, James: **Excavations at Hacılar,** vol. I-II

MELLINK, M.J.: **"Excavations at Karataş-Semayük in Lycia, 1963"** American, Journal of Archaeology. 68, 1964;
"Excavations at Karataş-Semayük, 1964" AJA, 69, 1965
"Excavations at Karataş-Semayük, 1965", AJA, 70, 1966
"Excavations at Karataş-Semayük 1966", AJA, 71, 1967

MELLINK, M. J.: **"The Royal Tombs at Alacahöyük. The Aegean and The Near East"**, Studies Present to Hetty Goldman, New York, 1956.

ORTHMANN, Winifred: **Die Keramik der Frühen Bronzezeit aus Inneranatolian,** Berlin, 1963

ÖZGÜÇ, Tahsin ve AKOK, M.: **Horoztepe,** TTK. Basımevi-Ankara, 1958.

ÖZGÜÇ, Tahsin: **"Yeni Araştırmaların Işığında Eski Anadolu Arkeolojisi".** Anatolia VII, 1963 (1964), 23-42.

ÖZGÜÇ, Tahsin: **"Çorum Çevresinde Bulunan Eski Tunç Çağı Eserleri"** TTK Belleten XLIV 175, 1980, s. 459-466.

ÖZGÜÇ, Tahsin: **"Kültepe Kazısında Bulunan Mermer İdol ve Heykelcikler",** Belleten, XXX. Sayı 81

ÖZGÜÇ, Tahsin: **"Yortan Mezarlık Kültürüne Ait Yeni Buluntular",** Belleten VIII, 1944

Uygarlıklar Ülkesi Türkiye 1985.

HISTORIC PERIODS
Assyrian Trade Colony Period
Old Hittite and Hittite Empire Periods

AKURGAL, E: **The Art of the Hittites,** London, 1962,

ALP, Sedat **Konya Civarında Karahöyük Kazılarında Bulunan Silindir ve Damga Mühürler"** T.T.K. Basımevi, Ankara, 1972

BERAN, T.: **Die Hethitische Giyptik von Boğazköy I.,** Berlin, 1967

BITTEL, K.: **Die Ruinen von Boğazköy,** Berlin ve Leipzig, 1937.

BITTEL, K: **Boğazköy-Hattuşa III. Funde aus der Grabungen 1952 1955,** Berlin, 1957

BITTEL, K.: **Boğazköy-Hattuşa II. Die Hethitischen Grabfunde von Osmankayası,** Berlin, 1958

BITTEL, K. ve NAUMANN, R.: **Boğazköy-Hattuşa,** Stuttgart, 1952

BITTEL K. - R. NAUMANN - S.Otto, Yızılıkaya, Architectur, Kelsbilder; Inschriften und Kleinfundevdeg 61, Berlin-1941

BITTEL, Kurt. **Die Hethiter Die Kunst Anatoliens Von Ende Des III.** Bis Zum Anfang Des I. Jahrtausends vor Christus. München, C.H. Beck, 1976

BLEGEN, C. W.: **Troy III. The Sixth Settlements,** Princeton, 1953
Troy IV. Settlements VII. and VIII, Princeton, 1958

EMRE, Kutlu: **"The Pottery of The Assyrian Colonies Period According to The Building Levels of the Kanish - Karum₁"** Anatolia (Anadolu) VII, 1963 (1964), s. 87-99

EMRE, Kutlu : **Anadolu Kurşun Figürinleri ve Taş Kalıpları,** T.T.K.VI. seri, 14, Ankara-1971

GARSTANG, J.: **The Hittite Empire,** London, 1929

GÜTERBOCK, Th. M.: **Guide to Ruins at Boğazkale,** Berlin, 1966

GÜTERBOCK, H.G.: **"Yazılıkaya",** Mittellungen der Deutschen Orientgesellschaft 86, 1953.

GÜTERBOCK, H. G.: **Halil Ethem Hatıra Kitabı,** Ankara, 1947

GÜTERBOCK, H.G. ve ÖZGÜÇ, N: **Ankara Bedesteninde Bulunan Eti Büyük Salonunun Kılavuzu,** İstanbul, 1946

KOŞAY, H.Z.: **Türk Tarih Kurmu Tarafından Yapılan Alacahöyük Harfiyatı,** Ankara 1938

KOŞAY, H.Z.: **Alacahöyük Kazısı 1936,** Ankara, 1944

KOŞAY, Hamit Z.: **Türk Tarih Kurumu Tarafından Yapılan Alacahöyük Kazısı** 1937-1939'daki Çalışmalara ve Keşiflere Ait İlk Rapor, T.T.K.Y., seri V, no.5 Ankara-1951

KOŞAY, Hamit Z - AKOK Mahmut: **Türk Tarih Kurumu Tarafından Yapılan Alaca Höyük Kazısı** 1940-1948'deki Çalışmalara ve Keşiflere Ait İlk Rapor, T.T.K.Y, seri V, no. 6, Ankara-1966'

LAMB, W: **"Excavations at Kusura Near Afyonkarahisar"**, Archaeologia, 86, 1937

LLOYD, S. ve MELLAART J.: **Beycesultan II,** London, 1965

LLOYD, S. - **Early Highland People of Anatolia,** London - 1947

OSTEN, H.H. von der: **The Alishar Höyük Seasons 1930-32, Part I** The University Chicago Press, Illinois, 1937

OSTEN, Hans H. : **The Alishar Hüyük. Season of 1927, I. The University of Chicago.** Oriental Institute Publications VI, Chicago-1930

ÖZGÜÇ, Tahsin: **Maşathöyük Kazıları ve Çevresindeki Araştırmalar** T.T.K.Y., Ankara-1973

ÖZGÜÇ, Tahsin: **Maşathöyük II,** T.T.K.Y., Ankara-1982

ÖZGÜÇ, Tahsin: **Kültepe-Kaniş II, Eski Yakındoğunun Ticaret Merkezinde Yeni Araştırmalar,** T.T.K.Y.V. dizi, sayı 41, Ankara 1986.

ÖZGÜÇ, Tahsin: **"VI. Trol'nin Anadolu Arkeolojisindeki Yeri",** Belleten X, 1946.

ÖZGÜÇ, Tahsin: **1948 Kültepe Kazıları,** Ankara, 1950

ÖZGÜÇ, Tahsin: **Kültepe-Kaniş,** Ankara, 1959

ÖZGÜÇ, Tahsin ve ÖZGÜÇ, Nimet: **1949 Kültepe Kazısı,** Ankara. 1953

ÖZGÜÇ, Tahsin: **"Bitik Vazosu",** Anatolia II (1957)

ÖZGÜÇ, Tahsin ve ÖZGÜÇ, Nimet: **1947 Karahöyük Kazısı,** Ankara, 1949

Late Hittite Period

Phrygian and Urartian Period

AKURGAL, Ekrem: **Phrygische Kunst,** A.Ü.D.T.C.F. yayınları, Ankara, 1955

AKURGAL, Ekrem: **Die Kunst Anatoliens,** Berlin 1961

AKURGAL, E.: **Spathethitische Bildkunst** Ankara, 1949

BALKAN, Kemal: **"Patnos'ta Keşfedilen Urartu Tapınağı ve Urartu Sarayı",** Atatürk Konferansları I, TTK. Basımevi, 1964

BERAN, T.: **Urartu, Kultur Geschichte des Alten Orient,** Stuttgart, 1961

BİLGİÇ, Emin-ÖĞÜN, Baki: **Adilcevaz Kef Kalesi Kazıları,** Anadolu 1965, Cilt 9, s.l.

BITTEL, K. ve OTTO, H.: **Demircihöyük. Eine vorgeschichtiche Ansiedlüng an der phrygisch-bithynischen Grenze,** Berlin, 1939

BOSSERT, ALKIM ve ÇABEL: **Karatepe Kazıları,** Türk Tarih Kurmu Basımevi, Ankara 1950

DELAPORTE, L.: **Malatya,** Paris, 1940

Elizabeth Simpson and Robert Payton, Royal Wooden : **Furniture from Gordion,** Archaelogy, volume 39. Number 6, s. 40, November, December. 1986.

GELB, Ignace: **Hittite Hieroglyphic Monuments,** Chicago-1939

ÖĞÜN, Baki: **Urartu Halk Mezarları,** Cumhuriyetin 50. Yıldönümü Anma Kitabı, Ankara Üniversitesi DTCF Yayınları, 1974.

ÖZGÜÇ Tahsin: **"Anıtkabir Tümülüsleri",** Belleten, X. Sayı 41

ÖZGÜÇ, Tahsin: **Altıntepe Mimarlık Anıtları ve Duvar Resimleri,** Ankara 1966.

ÖZGÜÇ, Tahsin: **Altıntepe II Mezarlar, Depo Binası ve Fildişi Eserler,** Ankara, 1969.

PIOTROVSKY, Boris B., The Ancient Civilization of Urartu, Geneva 1969.

PIOTROVSKY, Boris B., The Kingdom of Van and Its Art, Urartu, New York 1967.

TEMİZER, Raci: **"Ankara'da Bulunan Kybele Kabartması",** Anatolia VII, s. 179-182, 1959

TEMİZER, Raci: **"Kayapınar Höyüğü",** Belleten XVIII, 1954

VAN LOON : **Maurits Nanning; Its Distinctive Traits in the Light of New Excavations,** İstanbul 1966.

WOOLLEY, C.L.: **Carchemisch Part II, London-1921.**

WOOLLEY, C.L.: Carchemisch Part III. The Excavations In The Inner Town, Insriptions, London-1952.

YOUNG, R.S: **Three Great Early Tumuli,** University of Pennsylvania, 1981

YOUNG, R.S.: **"Gordion: Phrygian Construction and Architecture",** Expedition, The Bulletin of the University Museum of the University Pennsylvania.

YOUNG, R.S.: **Gordion Kazıları ve Müzesi Rehberi,** Ankara Turizmi Eski Eserleri ve Müzeleri Sevenler Derneği Yayınları

ANATOLIAN CIVILIZATIONS FROM THE 7th CENTURY B.C. ON

Akurgal. E.: **Die Kunst Anatoliens,** Berlin 1961; **Orient und Okzident** Baden-Baden 1966; **The Art of Greecese: The Orijins,** New York 1968; **Ancient Civılızatıons and Ruins of Turkey,** İstanbul 1985; **Griechische und Römische Kunst in der Turkei,** Hirmer 1987.

BEAN, G.E.: **Aegean Turkey,** London 1966

BOSCH, E.: **Quellen zur Geschichte der Stadt Ankara im Altertum,** T.T.K. Ankara 1967

COOK, J., **Ionia and the East,** London 1962

DUYURAN, R.,: **Batı Anadolu,** İstanbul 1948

ERZEN, A.,: İlk Çağda Ankara, Ankara 1946

EYİCE, Semavi: **Ankara'nın Eski Bir Resmi,** Ank. 1972

FOSS, C., **Late Antique and Byzantine,** Ankara, DOP 31, 1977

GALANTİ, Avram: **Ankara Tarihi** I-II, İst. 1946-1951

GÜLEKLİ, Nurettin Can: **Ankara Rehberi,** Ank. 1949

GÜLEKLİ, Nurettin Can: **Ankara Tarih ve Arkeoloji,** Ank. 1948

GÜLEKLİ, C. : **The guide of Ankara,** Ankara 1961

GÜRÜN,:Ceyhan: Türk Hanlarının Gelişimi ve İstanbul Hanları Mimarisi, Ankara 1978

Hamit Zübeyr Koşay: **"Ankara Arkeoloji Müzesinin İlk Kuruluş Safhası İle İlgili Anılar",** Belleten C. XLIII. S. 170 Ankara 1979

İnan, J. - Rosenbaum, E., Roman and Early Byzantine Portrait Soulpture in Asie Minör. Oxford 1966

KOŞAY, H.Z.: **Augustus Tempel in Ankara,** Anatolia 2, 1957

KRENCKER-SCHEDE.: Der Tempel in Ankara, Berlin 1936

MAHMUT, A.: **Ankara Roma Hamamı,** Türk Ark Derg. 17, 1968

ÖNEY, Gönül: **Ankara'da Türk Devri Dini ve Sosyal Yapıları,** Ankara 1972.

ÖZDEMİR, Rıfat: **XIX. Yüzyılın İlk Yarısında Ankara,** Ank. 1986

Publication of
The association for the support and encouragement of
the Museum of Anatolian Civilizations.